A Different Point of View

A Different
Point of View

Sara Jeannette Duncan

MISAO DEAN

McGill-Queen's University Press
Montreal & Kingston • London • Buffalo

© McGill-Queen's University Press 1991
ISBN 0-7735-0792-2

Legal deposit first quarter 1991
Bibliothèque nationale du Québec

Printed in Canada on acid-free paper

This book has been published with the help of a grant
from the Canadian Federation for the Humanities,
using funds provided by the Social Sciences and
Humanities Research Council of Canada.

Canadian Cataloguing in Publication Data

Dean, Misao
   A different point of view
   Includes bibliographical references.
   ISBN 0-7735-0792-2
   1. Duncan, Sara Jeannette, 1861-1922 – Criticism and
   interpretation. I. Title.
   PS8457.U626Z63 1991   C813'.4   C90-090342-2
   PR9199.2.C68Z63 1991

Typeset in 10.5/13 Palatino by Caractéra inc., Québec.

Contents

Acknowledgments

This study grew out of graduate work on Duncan, and I am indebted to the comments and inspiration provided by "the two Mathews" of Canadian literature: Robin Mathews, recently retired from Carleton University, who supervised my MA thesis on Duncan and remains a valued friend and respected teacher; and John P. Matthews of Queen's University, who allowed me to work on my Ph.D. thesis in an atmosphere of camaraderie and optimism. I feel privileged to have had the opportunity to learn from both. Leslie Monkman of Queen's University provided stimulating suggestions on larger directions for my thesis and much-needed moral support.

The Maxwell MacOdrum Library and the departments of English at Carleton University and the University of Ottawa have gracefully endured my presence there as a researcher and a sessional lecturer. I hope this study will justify the faith of my friends at both institutions. I would especially like to thank Enoch Padolsky, who first suggested the subject to me.

I would also like to thank Carl F. Klinck and Special Collections at the D.B. Weldon Library, University of Western Ontario, for allowing access to their collection of Duncan's play manuscripts.

Parts of this book have been published, in altered form, in *Re(dis)covering our Foremothers* (edited by Lorraine McMullen, University of Ottawa Press), as the Introduction to the Tecumseh Press edition of *A Daughter of Today*, and in *The Literary Criterion*.

I thank Maria Elena Lopez for providing loving child care for my infant daughter during the final stages of revision of this book.

Lindsay Mann contributed his time, his expertise in matters of style and logic, his patience, and his proofreading skills: "Gladly wolde he lerne and gladly teche." I am grateful for his support.

Abbreviations

AG *An American Girl in London*

CC *Cousin Cinderella*

Imp. *The Imperialist*

SA *Set in Authority*

TBO *The Burnt Offering*

A Different Point of View

Art lives upon discussion, upon
experiment, upon curiosity, upon variety
of attempt, upon the exchange of views
and the comparison of standpoints.
        Henry James, "The Art of Fiction"

A Different Point of View: The Colonial Perspective in Sara Jeannette Duncan's Novels

What makes Canadian writing Canadian? This question has interested readers and writers at least since the Confederation period, when Archibald Lampman suggested that our cold climate would not only produce a distinctive, striving spirit in literature but a whole new race. Attempts to identify a "tradition" in Canadian literature have often been frustrated by the facts of our colonial heritage: Canadian writers seldom took works by other Canadians as models, and the work of those who did was often judged to be inferior to the work of those who consciously emulated foreign models. Attempts to identify a paradigm or theme common to all Canadian creative writing have been hampered by the limitations of their own methodology; such approaches have often led to superficial readings that merely demonstrate how certain works may be "plugged in" to a model.

Many Canadian writers themselves confronted the question of the "Canadianness" of Canadian writing; Sara Jeannette Duncan was one of them. Born in Brantford, Canada West, in 1861, she grew up in a booming industrial centre that was, paradoxically, at the far edge of English-speaking intellectual life. She was two generations away from the Rebellion of 1837, when citizens from the Brantford area had formed a significant part of the homespun crew that scattered across Yonge Street, confusedly attending at "the making of a nation." She was one generation away from those august gentlemen in decent broadcloth who made Confederation; that event, and the nationalist literary and political flowering it inspired, provided the context for her own work. Her novels and journalism address themselves to the "difference" that her sex and ex-centric nationality allowed her to feel, to the question of what it means to be a colonial, to the colonial point of view.

"Point of view" was an important concept for late nineteenth-century novelists; Henry James, in his novels and his prefaces, argues that the choice of a point of view from which to tell the story is an important technical consideration that actually determines the story itself. With his famous analogy of the "House of Fiction" he suggests that the process of writing is like looking out a window onto the world; the choice of window limits what exactly the novelist sees, and to some extent how the novelist interprets truth. As modern ideas of subjectivity and scientific research developed (from about the 1880s onwards), scholars began to explore comparative religious studies, social engineering, and the "higher criticism," and to question long-accepted ideas. English-speaking readers came to accept that while truth exists, it is not always something that can be agreed upon; it depends upon your point of view.

Applying ideas drawn from James and other modern writers to her Canadian experience, Sara Jeannette Duncan envisaged a collective colonial point of view, created by the colonials' experience of living in, and of commitment to, life on the margins of Empire. Suspicion of British and American imperialist assumptions and respect for colonial independence were her Canadian inheritance; born at the height of the British Empire, Duncan herself had witnessed many examples of inflexible British administration as well as the first flowering of American militaristic belligerence. Duncan's marriage in 1891 to Everard Cotes, an Anglo-Indian civil servant, and her subsequent experience of life in Calcutta and Simla had shown her the connections between her Canadian experience and that of other colonials, and had confirmed her view that the colonial point of view on international affairs, while often overlooked by centrist legislators, usually offered the most practical solutions to local problems. Yet as a professional journalist (for *The Week*, the *Montreal Star*, and *The Globe*, among other newspapers), and later as a novelist, Duncan also saw herself as part of a monologic idealist tradition of literature in English that included Matthew Arnold and Thomas Carlyle. A vigorous and witty controversialist, she made no bones about her commitment to the future of the Empire and her personal identification with British history and British mission. Like many of her contemporaries, she saw the Empire as a bulwark against the destructive social effects of materialist capitalism; an effective check on us militarism; and a preserve for the ideals of justice, disinterested debate, altruism, and community which were threatened by the conditions of modern life. Her work speaks to the contradiction, as common among Canadians of her day as of ours, between commitment to the ideals of our European heritage and suspicion of its imperialist motives, to the difference that is the Canadian point of view.

Duncan's view of her position as a Canadian was intimately related to her view of her role as a woman. The nationalism of the 1880s that fostered Duncan's understanding of the colonial point of view coincided with the first organized feminist movement, in favour of women's suffrage (a coincidence that has been repeated in more recent history with the revival of both feminism and nationalism in the 1960s and 1970s).[1] Duncan's early declaration in favour of women's suffrage, like her belief in the legitimacy of Canada, again placed her on the margins of centrist ideology. As a woman, created and defined as "other" by malestream ideology, Duncan was aware that social, political, and literary conventions imposed artificial limitations on women, just as British colonial stereotypes placed artificial limits on Canadians. Moreover, her comments on the role of the heroine in the modern novel clarify her view that to write as a colonial in an international context is to write in a feminine voice. Her fellow Canadians consistently characterized their country as feminine; "Miss Canada" appeared in political cartoons and popular patriotic poetry next to England's "Mrs Britannia" and "John Bull," and the American "Cousin Jonathan" and "Uncle Sam."[2] Canada's lack of legal power in diplomatic affairs, its creation of cultural identity through relationship with "family members" – the us and England – and its emphasis on the mediating role in international politics characterize it as feminine.

The voice of colonial India, Duncan's adult home, was also feminine: popularly conceived of as the "bride of the Anglo-Saxon race," India was traditionally the passive field upon which the potent imperialist exercised his racial superiority. But here again Duncan's allegiances did not follow the imperial norm: her race identified her with the imperialist, yet her colonial orientation and her idealism made her sympathetic to the Indian movement for independence and to what she perceived as the contemplative, religious "oriental mind."

Like her nationalism, Duncan's feminism was also ambivalent: despite her allegiance to the colonial feminine, she was married and committed to living within patriarchal society. In her writing, she joined in the discourse of power and submission that was the essence of popular romantic fiction. As a woman and a colonial, she was "neither wholly 'subcultural' nor, certainly, wholly main-cultural, but negotiate[d] difference and sameness, marginality and inclusion in a constant dialogue."[3] In the overt political content and in the narrative strategies of her novels, Duncan presents a view from the margin of Anglo-American ideology, writing against the developing aesthetic and ideological traditions of imperialist patriarchy while fully implicated in them.

In *A Room of One's Own*, Virginia Woolf characterized the "double consciousness" of living both inside and outside British culture as typical of women, yet her description also captures the emotional relationship of the Canadian of British descent to England. Like Woolf, Duncan and her colonial characters confronted a civilization that assumed their loyalty without offering a significant return, that demanded their sacrifice without acknowledging their interests. Like Woolf, Duncan may have been "surprised by a sudden splitting off of consciousness, say in walking down Whitehall, when from being the natural inheritor of that civilisation, she becomes, on the contrary, outside of it, alien and critical."[4] The double consciousness of being female and Canadian yet middle class and British, an inheritor of British civilization yet alien from it, made Duncan "(ambiguously) nonhegemonic"[5] – non-hegemonic by virtue of her opposition to the dominant culture, but only ambiguously so, because by definition no one can be outside hegemony. Duncan could not be a whole-hearted nationalist because she was an imperialist, could not be an unqualified feminist because she finally accepted patriarchally imposed definitions of the female. Like most colonials, she struggled to integrate what she knew by virtue of her colonial experience with what she accepted of the discourse that defined her as object.

DUNCAN'S SUBTLE OPPOSITION to the status quo of British and American intellectual life in itself constituted her art as political, for both writer and reader. Although Duncan did not commit herself to a political program, much less to a specific political party, her insistence that the colonial point of view must be respected in international affairs as well as in sexual politics often offends modern readers trained to view such commitment as "rhetoric." Nevertheless, modern critics of Duncan's work have generally resisted the view that her novels primarily address political issues. The reason for this resistance may lie partly in the prevailing definition of the political novel. In his critical biography of Duncan, *Novelist of Empire*, Thomas Tausky adopts a definition of the political novel that follows the liberal distinction between form and content by focusing on the perceived political affiliation of the characters.[6] Tausky points out that only one of Duncan's novels clearly fits his definition, although by slightly loosening his criteria he discusses three novels in his chapter on Duncan's politics. But even the wider framework excludes *His Royal Happiness*, despite its clear criticism of American[7] democracy and its idealization of Canada. Nor can it include *The Simple Adventures of a Memsahib*, which challenges the patriarchal emphasis on heterosexual romantic love as the fulfilment of a woman's life. In *Redney*, her book on Duncan, Marian Fowler assumes a similar distinction between art and politics: she interprets Duncan's preoccupation with political themes in *The Consort* as a sign of her personal frustration and waning creative powers. Fowler opposes genuine motivation, which she identifies with passion, to politics: "Redney is using politics instead of passion to whip the muse ... now she merely shuffles through the old ritual dance." Fowler's use of the novels as evidence of personal dissatisfaction bordering on neurosis allows her to downplay the political content of Duncan's work to the point that she sees the focus of *The Imperialist* as simple nostalgia, "a long, lyrical love letter, addressed to Redney's family, to her home town, to her country."[8]

A more useful perspective on Duncan's novels is gained by placing them in the context of late-nineteenth-century English fiction by women. Many late-nineteenth-century women took to the novel as a platform for the dissemination of ideas about society, since almost all other intellectual occupations were closed to them. For the female intellectual or reformer, the novel was a natural medium for ideas. "As she and her contemporaries were fully aware, the novel was a medium for the expression of ideas about the society in which man lives. The vital issues of the day ... were also the issues of much of the fiction of her age ... No serious intellectual or practical issue, from the place of God in the universe to the effects on society of the development of cotton-weaving machines, eluded the nineteenth-century novelist ... [she] had a sense of mission, a categorical imperative to observe, to write, and to influence readers."[9] Like her contemporaries in Britain and the US, Duncan saw no contradiction between art and ideology, and unabashedly saw her art as that of "dramatizing" an effective "leading idea," as a medium for intellectual debate.

Moreover, in her novels, both the form and the content constitute political statement. Like those feminist writers who "write against the tradition," Duncan deliberately and self-consciously challenged the expected conventions of the romance novel in order to express her sense of the artificial limitations that the romance script imposes upon women in both narrative and society. Such challenges to convention (in both the aesthetic and the social senses of the word) announce her refusal to fit in to predetermined social and political categories. Such challenges to narrative conventions (and, by implication, social and ideological ones) are more readily found in authors who are doubly marginalized – by both their gender and their ethnic or national allegiances – and are "practices available to those groups – nations, subcultures, races, emergent social practices (gays?) – which wish to criticize, to differentiate from, to overturn the dominant forms of knowing and understanding."[10] The doubly marginalized narrator, made aware of "outsiderness" because both female and Canadian, is still joined to the ideological centre by her class, her education, and her race; "in marginalised dialogue with the orders she may also affirm."[11] Duncan worked from within the system by continuing to acknowledge the traditional norm as norm, yet asserting a different point of view.

The identification of Duncan as a doubly marginalized writer presupposes her allegiance to her sex and her nationality, but the idea that Duncan was consciously Canadian and a self-aware woman has traditionally been problematic for critics of her work. Duncan was born in Canada and began her career as a journalist contributing to the Toronto *Globe*, the *Washington Post*, the *Montreal Star*, and *The Week*. Her first book, *A Social Departure*, is a semi-fictional account of her trip around the world with fellow journalist Lily Lewis. Many of the foreign reviewers did not even notice that the narrator of the book was a Canadian; Duncan allowed Canada to fade into the background as her fictionalized persona left the CPR for a ship that took her to Japan, Southeast Asia, and India. Of the nineteen signed books that follow *A Social Departure*, sixteen make only token references to Canada, concentrating instead on life in London, New York, and Calcutta. Duncan's early years seem, at first glance, to have had very little impact upon her work.

The general critical response to Duncan's work has been governed by the fact of her international career. In 1893, Lampman was the first to congratulate "Miss Sara Jeannette Duncan" on having escaped the "small prospect of advancement"[12] in her native country in favour of the greener fields of Europe. (Lampman seems to have been unaware that Duncan had actually gone to India, a questionable career move.) Claude Bissell places her firmly in the "cosmopolitan" tradition in his introduction to *The Imperialist*,[13] and Lionel Stevenson remarks in *Appraisals of Canadian Literature* that Duncan "does not set out to interpret Canada either to her own inhabitants or to outsiders."[14] For these critics, the exclusion of most of Duncan's work from consideration as Canadian is based on a definition that prescribes a Canadian setting or significant Canadian characters. Tausky follows that definition when he remarks that "students of Canadian literature have little cause to love" Everard Cotes, the Anglo-Indian civil servant who married Duncan and introduced her to India and England; in his view, if Duncan had remained in Canada her work might have been "100% Canadian content," and so automatically of interest.

Judged by the criteria of setting or national identification of the characters, the works of Henry James would have scant claim to a place in American literature, and Joseph Conrad would arguably be undeserving of British notice. The cases for considering James as American and Conrad as British are based on viewpoint, literary influence, and philosophical background. If Canadian writing were considered similarly, as part of a canon of writing interesting in itself, to Canadians if to no one else, Duncan's work should not be included or excluded on the grounds of setting or character alone. Duncan's attitude to Canada, her sense of the rightness of Canadian habits and customs, her willingness to see Canadian personality as the norm or even the ideal, and the relation of her ideas to those of major Canadian thinkers are the real indicators of whether Duncan is a Canadian writer. Canadian criticism has perhaps suffered from the same marginality that Duncan revealed in her explorations of point of view; as part of a colonized minority ourselves, Canadian critics have only recently seen the possibility and the value of relating Duncan's work to that of her contemporaries in ways which suggest that it was part of a developing intellectual tradition.

Duncan's technique of employing a detached, ironic narrator further confuses attempts to identify her national allegiance. The narrator of *The Imperialist* (the only novel set in Canada) speaks in a superior and almost scientifically detached voice. This prompted Northrop Frye to quote a passage from the novel as a classic example of the author who refuses to advocate any position or to ally herself with any tradition: "Here is a voice of genuine detachment, sympathetic but not defensive either of the group or of herself, concerned primarily to understand and to make the reader see."[15] While for Frye ironic detachment from nationality is a sign of a mature writer, for other critics Duncan's irony is merely confusing. Michael Peterman remarks that Duncan's seeming lack of national orientation has in effect excluded her from consideration by American, British, or Canadian critics: "Much of the instability of her reputation today grows out of the fact that, because of her flexibility and cosmopolitan ease, she seemed in her time a homeless writer, one who could write trenchantly of India's political difficulties, of life in Parisian garrets, of social comedy in London and New York, but one who never clearly identified herself with a national literary tradition ... the 'delightful' manner in which she made use of the international theme, had the effect of de-nationalising her."[16]

Moreover, because modernism privileges cynical irony as a mode of seeing the real, for many critics Duncan's irony seems to be merely objective realism. The realism she drew from writers such as William Dean Howells and James thus contributes to the impression that her work is detached from, rather than politically engaged with, the issues of colony and empire. (Some critics have also implied that her interest in work of Howells and James made her fiction more American than Canadian). But Duncan's attitudes to realism and irony must be placed in the context of the intellectual dualism of the real and the ideal and the accompanying oppositions of democracy and authority, realism and romance, that dogged the nineteenth-century intellectual. Duncan, like many colonial writers, used irony as a technique to disguise her critique of the ideology of the centre. She relied on the reader to decipher the "parallax,"[17] the point of view from which her ironic statements would make sense, turning away from the chaotic implications of "romantic irony"[18] towards the ultimate meaning that idealist philosophy seemed to promise. Duncan's irony is not de-nationalizing, nor is it simply objective realism (though it may seem so to a modern reader), and confusion about these elements disappears when her ironic technique and her theory of realism are closely examined.

As A.B. McKillop, Leslie Armour, and Elizabeth Trott have argued, the characteristically Canadian response to the dualism of the ideal and the real was to try to reconcile the two. Duncan reconciled the perceived opposition of the real and the ideal through the popular version of idealism, derived from Carlyle and Arnold, which eventually came to dominate Canadian intellectual life and which persisted in Canada long after the rest of the English-speaking world had gone on to modernist materialism. Canadian intellectuals saw the material world as an embodiment of transcendent values whose significance could be brought out in realist fiction through careful selection of detail. While Duncan admired the realism of the Americans Howells and James, her own aim was quite different from what she saw as theirs: Duncan felt that Howells glorified life for the sake of its material commonplaces, while she went beyond the commonplace to show the representative significance of realistic details.

The idealism that underlies Duncan's novelistic method also provides a focus for addressing social issues such as the independence of the colonies, the institution of democratic government, universal education, and female suffrage. The version of idealism that became known through Carlyle's writings is essentially a framework that makes sense out of the chaotic revolutions of the nineteenth century: such change is not to be feared but rather welcomed as part of a general movement toward a predetermined and definitively good end. Social change is to be undertaken, with the ultimate ends of justice, peace, and equality in view, by changing institutions within a seemingly stable framework. British idealism, however, tended to focus on abstract ends rather than means, and so "turned right" with the more conservative politics of Carlyle and F.H. Bradley,[19] while Canadian idealism remained essentially a reformist philosophy which held that the real and the ideal existed equally. The struggle to make the real conform to the ideal through the secularization of religious thought[20] gave thinkers such as G.M. Grant, Agnes Maule Machar, and John Watson the inspiration to propose ameliorations of the materialist capitalism that they confronted. The "reorientation of the Canadian academic community towards idealism,"[21] which took place at the end of the nineteenth century and the beginning of the twentieth, quickly became a popular reorientation as well, as thinkers such as Machar, Watson, and Paxton Young became influential through their numerous publications and involvement in the training of Presbyterian clergy and the formation of the United Church.

The legitimacy of the individual which the reconciliation of realism and idealism suggested to Canadians provided a philosophical basis for Canadian autonomy within the wider community suggested by the Imperial Union movement. Imperial union, based on the idealist conception of diverse physical manifestations of a universal truth, would allow for a peaceful federation of contending nationalities and a wider union of the human race, but would still allow for the individuality of the various member countries. For Canadians such as Duncan, a united empire would reconcile the two important needs of political man: the need for self-government and the need to look up to an ideal example. With these two principles firmly in view, individual nations could move to material prosperity without giving up the human goals of charity, political stability, and universal education. Duncan applied the standard she derived from her Canadian experience and from the Canadian view of empire in her descriptions of the social and physical conditions of the us, Canada, England, and India, and attempted to show how the fullest development of individuality could be achieved through recognition of the highest good.

Duncan's interest in and support of the Imperial Federation movement is another factor that lends support to the idea that she thought of herself as a particularly Canadian citizen of Empire. Robert Grant Haliburton calls the United Empire Loyalists the first imperial federationists, on the grounds that they suffered and died for the ideal of the unity of the race even while they were betrayed by British policy.[22] Carl Berger suspects that the claim that Canadians originated imperial federation was a myth,[23] created by the nationalist stream of the Imperial Federation movement to increase their sense of moral superiority to both Britain and the US; on the other hand, George Parkin, one of the most influential Canadian imperialists, stated categorically that "Imperial Federation is of Colonial – not of English – origin."[24] (One is tempted to add that, as the most famous spokesman for the movement, he should know.)

The "popular idealist" philosophy so influential in Canadian conceptions of a united empire also suggested a rationalization for the movement towards self development for women. The ideal of womanhood, including her "moral superiority" to men and her ability to create and maintain peaceful relations among family members, was traditionally embodied in the role of homemaker and bearer of children. Duncan, however, influenced by the "maternal feminists" (who advocated the extension of women's maternal role into social policy) and the ideology of the "new woman," portrayed the ideal as embodied in a new generation of women pursuing their best impulses in a felt vocation for higher education and professions. The ideal remained the same, but its embodiment changed.

While Duncan's idealism and her support for the federation of the British Empire suggest her agreement with her contemporaries on the composition of the Canadian point of view, the particular form in which she represented the eventual union of the Empire shows the influence of her feminism. She rejected the idea that male-dominated systems of trade and government are sufficient to create peaceful relations between the countries of the Empire, and used the metaphors of family alliances between parent and child, husband and wife, to illustrate the bonds of "sentiment" which must exist between nations in order to promote peace and prosperity. The male characters in Duncan's books attempt to unite the Empire using the tools of trade and diplomacy, but the female characters actually unite the Empire with the tangible ties of marriage and children. Women traditionally have a special duty in the family to promote affection and understanding among the members, and this duty becomes a public one as women fulfill a special role in the Empire, creating the affectionate ties that are the most important part of diplomatic alliances and bind countries to support each others' interests.

The preservation of affectionate ties between races, classes, and nations, as between individuals, is the moral constant in Duncan's portrayal of political rivalries, one that recent feminist scholarship has identified as constitutive of feminine psychology as created in the nuclear family. Nancy Chodorow's description of the daughter's creation of identity through relationship with others, rather than through separation and independence, suggestively recalls Duncan's portrayal of a kind of colonial self-government that unites the values of independence from and connection to England. Carol Gilligan's corollary research into women's moral decisions suggests that women consistently choose to maintain relationships rather than to pursue abstract concepts of good and evil. Duncan's characterization of the nations of the Empire as "one race" who cannot and must not be separated by abstractions "of so little consequence as a form of government"[25] similarly seems to connect to Gilligan's ideas about characteristically feminine traits as produced in the nuclear family.[26] Thus Duncan's ideas about women, about the Empire, and about nationhood seem to reflect her feminism and her femininity.

Duncan often used the metaphor of marriage to symbolize alliances between countries, but she also portrayed actual international marriages that gave women power as inter-cultural interpreters and bearers of family wealth. Creating India as "the bride of the Anglo-Saxon race" was a cliché of orientalist discourse, but Duncan wrote against the stereotype by showing that the alliance with British law would bring the Eastern bride not protected passivity but independence, education, and relief from abuse. The Canadian bride, such as Advena Murchison in *The Imperialist* or Mary Trent in *Cousin Cinderella*, gains power through her ability to bestow the dowry that represents her nation: wealth, a field for action, and the possibility of a new social harmony. The American bride in Duncan's later books brings the healing of the schism between Britain and the US and the possibility of fruitful alliance in time of war. In Duncan's books, as the narrator states in *The Simple Adventures of a Memsahib*, "Feminine connections ... [are] the only sort which are really binding"[27] between nations.

DUNCAN'S POLITICAL VIEWS were often those of a small-c conservative, but her belief in social reform and women's suffrage and her attacks on colonialism and entrenched privilege belie a simple identification with any one party. George Lukacs points out that movements that oppose bourgeois democracy on the basis of a

communitarian ideal often blur party lines: "The opposition movements ... always run the danger of swinging over from a left to a
right-wing criticism of bourgeois democracy, i.e. from dissatisfaction with *bourgeois* democracy to opposition to *democracy in general.*
If one, for instance, follows the careers of ... important writers like
Bernard Shaw, one sees ... zigzag movements of this kind from
one extreme to the other."[28] During Duncan's lifetime, political lines
in Britain and Canada were extremely fluid. Both Benjamin Disraeli
and Joseph Chamberlain began their careers as Radicals and ended
as Tories; Disraeli and Herbert Henry Asquith both considered
forming governments of efficiency or reconciliation that would do
away with party lines. Carlyle's ideas were variously associated
with the right and the left, and the Fabians flirted with eugenics
and fascism as well as with democratic socialism. In Canada, the
Canada First movement began by opposing all party divisions as
inefficient and petty; it ended by forming its own party. The Liberal
Party of Canada seesawed between support for commercial union
and imperial federation. Duncan is often called a conservative, but
during her lifetime she remained friends with John Willison, editor
of a Liberal paper. She admired and quoted John Stuart Mill and
Arnold; she upheld the free market system but also supported
relief payments to the poor. The political philosophy she espoused
eventually became the basis of the CCF.[29]

Duncan's political stance might more constructively be defined
within that elusive (and largely extinct) Canadian ideology, red
toryism. The red tory believes in a natural social hierarchy similar
to the one described in *The Imperialist* and the maintenance of that
hierarchy in a flexible way in the interests of preserving order. The
red tory also believes, generally, in progress and social reform, but
with the limit that man is probably not perfectable. Increases in
personal freedom are not necessarily progressive (as Duncan maintained when she argued that the aim of the movement for women's
rights is not freedom in itself); progress, for the red tory, consists
in restraining the more vicious human traits to prevent the victimization of the weak – in practical terms, state legislation to restrain
capitalism. The red tory thus shares with the socialist a belief in
the necessity of state intervention based on a collectivist view of
the social good, the view that Pamela Pargeter comes to when she
campaigns on behalf of the Labour Party in *The Consort.* In Canada,
red tories and their socialist allies have historically been the basis

of the nationalist movement; red tory nationalists have generally fought modern liberal capitalism (the descendant of Mill's utilitarianism), and so have fought Canada's incorporation into the US economic empire.

Red toryism, or "tory radicalism," has been a major factor in the intellectual history of Canada.[30] Gad Horowitz accounts for the differences between Canadian and US culture by the "touch of toryism" that survived the homogenizing influence of North American liberalism. He believes that the dominant liberal ideology in Canada is "considerably mitigated by a tory presence initially and a socialist presence subsequently." He agrees that the two are fundamentally connected by a "corporate-organic-collectivist" view of society, which is the result of the "non-Liberal British elements" that have entered "into English-Canadian society *together* with American liberal elements at the foundations." Of course it would be an exaggeration to claim self-conscious political radicalism for nineteenth-century Canadian conservatives. But certainly the "pink toryism" that Robin Mathews claims for Susanna Moodie was the ideology of a significant minority. Like Duncan, Moodie "supported meritocracy. She moved toward the breakdown of class as it was defined in Europe. She rejected individualism and – in a not fully articulated way – capitalist exploitation." Like Moodie, Duncan may be called a pink tory: "pro-British in culture, pro-Canadian in aspirations for the future, socially committed to community and responsibility and, therefore, fearful of individualist, republican 'democracy.'"[31]

The pink tory was often an imperialist. Support for the strengthening of ties between the self-governing nations of the British Empire was one strategy for combatting materialism and deterioration of social bonds.[32] The Empire was supposed to be held together by ideals that transcended the profit motive, and to be motivated by the desire to do good works by bringing the benefit of British civilization to the "lesser breeds without the law." While acknowledging that the Empire was originally an instrument for money-making, Canadian imperialists saw the future of the Empire in the preservation of the ideals embodied in British history. G.M. Grant declared that the mission of man was "to think great thoughts, to do great things, to promote great ideals," and to overcome "the vulgar and insolent materialism of thought and life, which is eating into the heart of our people."[33] To this end, Canadian imperialists took Carlyle's suggestion to 'work thou in well-doing,' infusing the concept of secular work with religious enthusiasm. Support for the Empire seemed to provide the ideals and the opportunity for work (in the governing of dependencies and the building of new nations), as well as an economic mechanism for resisting the dominating influence of the quintessential materialists, the Americans.

The pink tory, if she was a woman, was also often a suffragist, for the majority of the members of the Canadian suffrage movement were politically conservative reformers, not revolutionaries. The radical call for the vote, which was founded in the belief in the essential equality of women, was rejected by the majority of the maternal feminist suffragists. They called for the vote as a first step toward necessary social reforms, such as temperance laws, legislation to give mothers equal custody of their children, and welfare and unemployment relief, that would "clean house" for the nation.[34]

One of the earliest women journalists to call for the ballot (in her *Globe* columns of 1885), Duncan agreed that most women would prefer to marry and have children, and she consistently depicted female characters in her novels who are "formed" for marriage. Yet she argued for the goal of women's financial and moral independence from men and for freedom of choice for women who felt the drive toward higher education and professions. Asserting that women had grown strong enough to bear the responsibility of the ballot, she demanded that they be treated as adults, with both the duties and responsibilities of citizens. She argued that women are as individual as men in their aptitudes and capabilities, and that their different callings and vocations must be respected. Chafing against the artificial legal strictures placed on women made her aware of the literary restrictions: those which created the passive heroine, the love story, the flirt, and always, always, a marriage at the end. Her ability to question stereotypes in life broadened to include a questioning of much received opinion.

This study will argue that, despite their ironic narrative voice and their technique of realistic dramatization, Duncan's novels and her journalism[35] present a political exposition and critique of the dominant ideologies of imperialism, unrestrained capitalism, bourgeois democracy, and patriarchy, and a program for social reform based upon ideas that she drew from her Canadian intellectual roots and her experience as a woman. In all her work, Duncan wrote from a different point of view, one that consciously differed from the received wisdom of the imperial centre yet included it as norm; she wrote as a colonial both committed to and different from the empire that created her.

CHAPTER TWO

The Colonial Narrator
and the Imperial Reader:
Reaching "Just Conclusions
upon Very Slight Data"

Near the beginning of *An American Girl in London* Mamie Wick, seated beside a forbidding-looking Englishwoman at dinner, exclaims to the reader: "You may imagine my feelings – or rather, as you are probably English, you can't." Mamie's remark displays Duncan's characteristic interest in wordplay that exploits the differences between North American and British English – "You may imagine my feelings" versus "You can't imagine my feelings." But she also evokes and ridicules a stereotype common to many colonial texts: that of the arrogant Briton who is literally unable to understand another point of view. A colonial reader who brings to the statement first-hand knowledge of the self-centred Briton's patronizing manner understands Mamie's words immediately. The colonial reader reconstructs the experience of imperial arrogance and agrees that such arrogance is ridiculous. Mamie's message is complicated, however, by the fact that her reader, as she states, is "probably English." Irony conventionally excludes its victim – in this case the arrogant British reader who is unable to sympathize with the colonial point of view.

Duncan addressed an audience that could seldom be expected to share her point of view. She published her books in England and the United States and often self-consciously directed her remarks to British or American readers; such readers would have brought to her text expectations about political and literary issues that were foreign to her. As a Canadian and a woman, Duncan was doubly removed from the ideological centre of the societies she addressed; as part of the Anglo-Indian community of Calcutta and Simla, fearful of the "subject races" and accused of luxury, feudalism, and racism by the opposition benches in Parliament, she possessed a point of view on imperial politics and colonial society that would not be shared by most of her readers. Although she was an outsider by virtue of her nationality and her sex, however, Duncan was also joined to the imperial ideological centre by her race, her class, her sense of participation in the English literary tradition, and her idealist support for the British Empire. In order to express colonial reality, Duncan negotiates the space between realism and idealism to create both representative and realistic character, conventional and unconventional narrative. Duncan also expresses her commitment to the colonial point of view through irony, adopting strategies that allow her to covertly criticize the assumptions of the ideological centre without betraying her own or her reader's allegiance to them.

As Lorraine Weir points out in her work on women writers, "Those who ... have endured centuries of colonization learn to value the riddling utterance above all."[1] Ironic writing disguises meanings that are unfamiliar or threatening to a dominant group by leaving out a central term that only the appropriate reader, who shares the experience of colonization, can fill in. According to Weir, women's texts "rely upon the harmonics of a hidden subtext, an unspoken system played by the text in the ear of an appropriately programmed reader in whom the subtext is systematically evoked."[2] Thus texts by women often seem like nonsense to readers who lack experience of feminine concerns, and are dismissed by the dominant culture as flawed.[3]

Irony that requires the hermeneutical task of filling in the blanks is also typically Canadian, Weir argues, by virtue of our psychological and economic colonization: "If women's texts are to the texts of patriarchy as Canada is and was to America and Britain, then it will not surprise us that much of the best writing in Canada exemplifies the strategies, and often the thematics as well, of women's texts."[4] Elaine Showalter also makes an explicit connection between the literatures of political colonies and writing by women in a male-dominated society, arguing that works by women must be seen "in relation to the ways in which any minority group finds its direction of self-expression relative to the dominant society."[5] Showalter's terminology is problematic for any student of Canadian literature; she lumps together black Americans, women, Jewish Americans, Canadians, and the colonizing minority of Anglo-India

– groups whose repossession of their cultures involves a very different mix of political and psychological factors. Nonetheless, writers from these groups share a voice that expresses both the colonizer's view and the subversive criticism of the oppressed.[6]

All of these readings of irony rely on Wayne Booth's description of the way in which irony draws readers into communities and excludes outsiders. Booth describes the process of reading "stable irony" as one that engages the reader in an active search for the "assumptions, often unstated, that ironists and readers share."[7] The reader experiences irony, according to Booth, as an invitation to join the author and a community of "sound readers" by rejecting the literal sense of the ironic statement and correctly reinterpreting it. Thus irony has the effect of consolidating a sense of community among those readers with the inside knowledge necessary to decipher it: "Often the predominant emotion when reading stable ironies is that of joining, of finding and communing with kindred spirits."[8] In this sense, irony as a technique becomes political; rather than simply calling for the reader's participation in solving a kind of linguistic puzzle, irony takes this process one step further by calling on the reader to recognize herself as part of a community of readers who share the inside joke with the author. Deciphering irony is thus an individual recognition of membership in a community, be it a general community of sound readers as Booth describes, or, in the case of colonial irony, a community of the politically or socially disenfranchised in the process of discovering a unique identity.

Moreover, Booth states that irony implies a sense of superiority in the ironist and the discerning reader and the victimization of the reader who is naive enough to take ironic statements at face value. The "correct" interpretation of stable irony thus implies the creation of victims. Booth downplays the resentment that irony implies, arguing that "the building of amiable communities is often far more important than the exclusion of naive victims."[9] In Duncan's novels, however, the creation of victims of irony is often central, and the victims are usually representatives of imperial power. The reader's task is thus to avoid being a victim of her irony – a difficult one, perhaps, for a British or American reader whose assumptions are essentially those that are being ridiculed. Perhaps the recurrence of such victims in Duncan's novels is the source of accusations by critics that Duncan revels in her sense of superiority and is "a terrible snob."[10] The text itself encourages the reader to separate herself from the ridiculous views of the imperial centre, and so encourages adoption of a different point of view on the politics of colonized societies.

APPLICATION of Weir's hermeneutical irony to Duncan's novels might be attacked on the grounds that Duncan seems to struggle with the depiction of the modern view of the world – a view characterized by a "romantic irony"[11] in which meaning is indeterminate because the truth is in flux, always in the process of becoming, and never clear. The indeterminacy of ironic meaning and, some would say, the impossibility of accurately reconstructing intended meanings render such ideas as "stable irony" useless. Many critics, including Michael Peterman, Clara Thomas, Carole Gerson, Francis Zichy and Thomas Tausky, have argued that the ironic tone of Duncan's fiction makes the determination of an authorial point of view difficult, if not impossible, and undermines the judgments stated in the novels.[12] Duncan, however, wrote within a tradition that regarded irony not as a world view but as a device to enhance meaning. The Victorians, especially those influenced by Thomas Carlyle, tended to turn away from the despair of meaninglessness implied by an ironic world view towards the positive choice depicted in Carlyle's *Sartor Resartus*. For followers of Carlyle's work the world is chaotic but still governed teleologically by a clear movement towards a positive goal. For Duncan, as for Carlyle, the fact that the world seems chaotic to humans shows only our faulty vision, not a faulty universe, and the ironic reversals in her stories depict the human struggle to see the truth, not the impossibility of truth itself.[13]

Duncan uses irony as a device to persuade the sympathetic and to ridicule the arrogant; she invites the reader to join in the colonial point of view by reconstructing the values that lie behind the ironic voice. Similarly, Henry James, one of the American authors Duncan was most familiar with, describes his irony as dependent upon an implied value system that the reader is invited to reconstruct: "The strength of applied irony being surely in the sincerities, the lucidities, the utilities that stand behind it. When it's not a campaign, of a sort, on behalf of the something better (better than the obnoxious, the provoking object) that blessedly, as is assumed, *might* be, it's not worth speaking of ... It implies and projects the other case, the case rich and edifying where the actuality is pretentious and vain."[14] Like James, Duncan relied on the reader to reconstruct "the sincerities, the lucidities, the utilities" that lay behind the "pretentious and vain" actuality. Duncan's irony is not modern skepticism but, rather, a technique that invites the reader to reconstruct the value system that lies behind it.

Successful creation of the meaning of ironic statements in Duncan's novels depends on two classes of information: public information available to any competent reader (such as topical references, historical information, literary stereotypes such as the "American Girl" or the "happy ending") as well as the private information gained from the experience of living as a colonial and a woman. Knowledge of the war over realism waged by Howells in the columns of US magazines, knowledge of the stereotypical "international" novel and the plots of popular romances, knowledge of specific historical events and figures – all conduce to a better understanding of Duncan's irony. But, more important, knowledge of imperial-colonial relations from the point of view of the colony, and of historical events in the life of the colony, is often necessary for a full understanding of the political implications of Duncan's technique. For example, in *A Social Departure*, Orthodocia asks S.J.D.[15] to define the "seepiar" and receives an ironical response: "The CPR ... is the most masterly stroke of internal economy a Government ever had the courage to carry out, and the most lunatic enterprise a Government was ever foolhardy enough to hazard. It was made for the good of Canada, it was made for the greed of contractors. It has insured our financial future, it has bankrupted us for ever. It is our boon and our bane. It is an iron bond of union between our East and our West – if you will look on the map you will discover that we are chiefly east and west – and it is an impotent strand connecting a lot of disaffected provinces. This is a coalition Liberal-Conservative definition of the CPR" (10). The key to decoding these contradictory statements is a knowledge of the scandals and the rhetoric surrounding the building of the Canadian Pacific Railway – knowledge that a Canadian could hardly fail to have in the late 1880s, but that an informed and sympathetic Briton might have as well. Without such knowledge, the narrator's travelling companion Orthodocia finds comprehension impossible. The conversation excludes and ridicules Orthodocia for her ignorance, but includes the narrator and her sympathetic readers.

Duncan's definition of the "seepiar" not only points out the contradictory nature of Canadian politics but also implies the impossibility of casually defining our history for an unselfconscious member of an imperial culture. Canadians (and those with knowledge of Canada) will understand; those who don't can hardly be made to understand, especially if they are English. The definition assumes a set of insiders and a set of outsiders, and Orthodocia's answer, "I'm sure it doesn't matter," merely confirms S.J.D.'s assumption that Orthodocia wants only enough information to take advantage of the system and not to understand it. Duncan's ironical diatribe thus includes the Canadian reader in a display of superior knowledge and makes Orthodocia the butt of a colonial joke. The narrator, in assuming the colonial perspective, has written the joke self-consciously to include both colonials and sympathetic Britons; the reader is thus encouraged to adopt her own "inside-outside" position to identify with the colonial and laugh at herself.

As this example illustrates, the use of irony constantly brings to the fore the question of communication itself. Can the characters communicate with each other, and can their communication be a model for understanding between the narrator and the reader? Mamie Wick's awareness of the differences between North American and British English does not always help her to understand her English friends. The irony of *An American Girl in London* is created by her retrospective awareness of what she did not, at the time, understand. As Mamie retells her story, the reader and the narrator understand better than the characters themselves what is going on between them.

Mamie Wick consciously addresses the expectations of a British reader when she introduces herself in the first chapter.[16] She makes her first statement, "I am an American girl," in order to explain any deviation she represents from the British norm: "I have observed, since I came to England, that this statement, made by a third person in connection with any question of my own conduct, is always broadly explanatory" (1). She introduces herself by way of her family history because she knows the British reader expects it. But Mamie hastens to point out that she was not born with the knowledge of how to communicate with the British; she has arrived at it through curious experiment and painful experience. She regards herself ironically as she tells the story of her own "cross questions and crooked answers" among the English.

Mamie's retrospective ability to decipher irony is indicated early in the novel when she overhears a group of pompous fellow-passengers from Boston discussing her: "One of them took up a position several miles behind her spectacles, looked at me through them, and then said something to her neighbour about 'Daisy Miller,' which the neighbour agreed to. I know what they meant now" (12). Mamie has acquired what the reader must already have to make sense of the passage: a knowledge of James's famous example of the literary type, the "American Girl." Like the reader, Mamie refers the statement to its literary source and concludes, correctly, that her Bostonian acquaintances are criticizing her independent and unconventional behaviour.

Mamie's conversations with her English friends, Lady Torquilin and Charlie Mafferton, highlight the problems in establishing communication between two cultures. Their first misunderstanding is over the use of the word "bad," which Lady Torquilin intends as a reference to Mamie's health and Mamie understands as an inquiry into the state of her soul (13). Throughout their conversations Lady Torquilin must ask, "Do you intend that for a joke?" (15), and Mamie must learn the meanings of "those English descriptive terms by which you mean something that you do not say" (236). But, most important, Mamie misunderstands Lady Torquilin's hints and Charlie Mafferton's attentions toward her. Mamie has men friends at home, with whom she shops and corresponds (such as Mr Winterhazel, who is perhaps named after James's Winterbourne), and so has no suspicions that Mafferton intends marriage. But the alert reader, who refers Mafferton's actions to the conduct of generations of Englishmen in novels from Jane Austen onwards, recognizes that a young man who gives up his tea for a walk and details the names, ages, and pursuits of his siblings before they are introduced has serious intentions. When Lady Torquilin tries to have a heart-to-heart talk with Mamie about Lord Mafferton's reaction to Charlie's interest in her, Mamie has no idea what the subject of the conversation is; to her it is simply gibberish. Lady Torquilin exclaims:

"What he'll have to say about it, heaven only knows! But Charlie is quite capable of snapping his fingers at him."

I was immensely interested. "What has Mr Mafferton been doing?" I asked.

"I've no reason to believe he's done it yet," said Mrs Torquilin, a little crossly I thought. "Perhaps he won't."

"I'm sure I hope not," I returned. "Mr Mafferton is so nice that it would be a pity if he got into trouble with his relations, especially if one of them is a lord."

"Then don't let him!" said Mrs Torquilin, more crossly than before.

"Do you think I would have any influence with him?" I asked her. "I should doubt it very much. Mr Mafferton doesn't strike me as a person at all susceptible to ladies' influence. But, if I knew the circumstances, I might try."

"Oh come along child!" Mrs Torquilin returned, folding up the napkin. "You're *too* stupid. I'll see the Maffertons in a day or two, and I'll tell them what I think of you." (72)

The innocent Mamie persists in believing that Mafferton's attentions to her and Lady Torquilin are a peculiar sort of British politeness, and she finds his suggestive remarks about his family connections and his plans for the future merely boring. But the narrator, who has survived the social consequences of her mistake, carefully preserves each of her mistakes in print and so allows the reader to decipher the irony.

The narrator of Duncan's *Cousin Cinderella* is herself a reader of the conversations that take place around her, and in demonstrating the process of arriving at "just conclusions upon very slight data" (303) creates a model for reading Duncan's irony. The voice of Mary Trent combines an understanding of the view of a partisan colonial (represented in the novel by her brother Graham) and enough understanding of the good intentions of the British to allow her to fill in the values that are left out of their conversation. Mary's sensitivity to cross-cultural communication allows the multiple meanings of words and their possible ironic interpretations to become one of the major themes in *Cousin Cinderella*; as Mary explains, "Clever people often unconsciously convey themselves so much more clearly than stupid, literal ones do, though using exactly the same words" (100).

In *Cousin Cinderella*, the interpretation of statements by both the British and the Canadians is dependent on a culturally based point of view, something that the Canadians are made aware of by their

difference from the British.[17] The point of view that characterizes
the Canadian narrator, Mary Trent, and her brother Graham was
formed by their upbringing in Canada. Graham tells Mary, "Now,
we with our empty country and our simple record, we've got a
point of view" (149) – a set of values different from those of the
British, which, he feels, allows Canadians in England to see more
and different things than the English themselves. Mary Trent associates the English point of view with "fog" – a fog of history,
tradition, and expectations that obscures a clear view of the present.
She tells Peter Doleford that England is "nearer heaven than any
other country. And I think if it weren't for the fogs you would all
see that it was" (248). The future of England is summed up in the
metaphor of a funeral procession in Kensington Square, wandering
in the fog and "pining away after Thackeray" (186).

The communication difficulties caused by the two points of view
are apparent in Graham's conversation with Lady Lippington, a
British aristocrat who has undertaken a campaign of society din-
ners and string-pulling to have her husband appointed governor-
general of Canada. Lady Lippington has good intentions; she
knows her husband is well-suited to the job of governor-general,
and, when the prickly Graham meets Lord Lippington, he agrees.
Lady Lippington intends to flatter Graham, yet he refuses to fill
in the blanks of Lady Lippington's intention in order to facilitate
communication.

Mary reports the conversation:

"Canada," [Lady Lippington] said, "has the greatest fascination for me.
Its history thrill-lls me; its loyalty touches me to the heart."

It seemed a good deal to say, in public like that; still, I didn't see why
it should have irritated Graham. But it did always, any reference to Canadian loyalty upon the lips of the aristocratic classes. He got so, at last,
that he preferred to hear them charge us with selfishness and sedition.

"That would greatly gratify Canada," he replied, "if she knew."

It sounded polite, but it was really temper; and I was thankful to see
that Lady Lippington perceived only the sound. That was the worst of
Graham in England; you never could depend upon his taking things the
way he was meant to take them. Luckily it was not often noticed that he
didn't; so I suppose no harm was done. (91–2)

Graham chooses the "riddling utterance," indicating to the colonial listener that Canada couldn't care less what Lady Lippington thinks. Only Mary detects the real meaning of Graham's seeming politeness: his frustration with Lady Lippington's assumption that Canada remains loyal despite British indifference. Mary also "riddles" the reader who has no experience of colonial frustration; only a sympathetic reader can guess why Graham "got so, at last, that he preferred to hear them charge us with selfishness and sedition." But, unlike most of the Britons that Graham victimizes with his ironic jabs, Mary also knows how Graham was meant to take Lady Lippington's remark, and expresses her frustration with his refusal to make allowance for good intentions, however ignorant. Mary offers a model for reading both sides of colonial-imperial communication.

Ability to know "whether one were joking" (113), to step into the colonial point of view as the reader of the novel must do, becomes an indicator of potential friendship for the Canadian brother and sister during their stay in London. One reason Mary feels so comfortable with her American friend, Evelyn Dicey, is that she, too, catches Graham's ironic jokes. Evelyn enjoys Graham's "chaffing her head off" (76) throughout their initial conversation, and she exclaims: "It just does my heart good to hear you talk. I've been among these sweet British for two solid months now, and they are darlings; but they don't exactly catch on, do they?" (71). Later, when Graham, Mary, and Evelyn enjoy a nostalgic Christmas turkey (with cranberries) at the Trent flat, Mary and Evelyn indulge their weariness of British incomprehension. Mary comforts Evelyn on the basis of their common continental ability to see the joke. "But never mind, Evie. Let them laugh at us as much as they can. We can laugh at them a great deal more, because we're made that way and they aren't, are they?" (213)

Among the British, the only individual who seems to catch on is Lord Peter Doleford. Mary notices that Lady Barbara persistently misunderstands Graham's ironic comments, but she feels sure that Doleford would be more responsive: "He would know, infallibly, whether one were joking" (113). Mary's impression is based on her conversations with Doleford about British ignorance of Canada, in which he admits that "the old tales, you know, of the Elizabethan explorers – they stick in our heads" and prevent anything more modern from taking hold (139). Although even Doleford proves to be "one of those Englishmen who always suppose that people mean exactly what they say," he manages to learn from Mary how to arrive "at just conclusions upon very slight data" (303). Doleford is the only one of his family adept enough at reading irony to reconstruct the tortured motives behind the engagement between Barbara and Graham, and he joins with Mary in condemning it. The eventual marriage between Mary and Peter, a union of love and equality, seems to join the two characters with the best hopes of continuing imperial-colonial cross-cultural communication, symbolizing the necessary reorganization of the Empire on the principles of equality and cultural sensitivity.

In *The Imperialist*, the narrator's colonial point of view allows her to create a realistic portrait of Elgin, Ontario, by acknowledging and then challenging the British reader's preconceptions about stories and about Canada. The novel opens with a description of Mother Beggarlegs, the ancient woman who sells gingerbread in the Elgin market square. British social convention demands a formal introduction to the lady; literary conventions derived from the eighteenth-century novel also prescribe a formal introduction by way of a genealogy. As Mamie Wick discovers in Britain, the English reader expects an account of a character's past and present history: "I have learned that in England you like to know a great deal about people who are introduced to you – who their fathers and mothers are, their grandfathers and grandmothers, and even further back than that" (AG, 3). But the narrator of *The Imperialist* protests, "It would have been idle to inquire into the antecedents" of Mother Beggarlegs; she belongs to a society so new that such information is often unobtainable and irrelevant. The "antecedents or even the circumstances, of old Mother Beggarlegs" are lost in history; what places her for the residents of Elgin is the Canadian indicator of social class: her occupation, which "was clear."[18] In her description of Mother Beggarlegs, the narrator links the conventions of the literary biography and British society and then dismisses them as irrelevant, showing the inadequacies of the old view in creating a realistic portrait of a different place.

The narrator recognizes the views of both the British reader and the colonial when she describes the attitudes of two recent immigrants to Elgin, John Murchison and Dr Drummond. She tells in some detail how the two came to Canada and explains their attitude to Britain with the exactness of one aware that she is talking to an audience with its own ideas of Canadian loyalty. "A sentiment of

affection for the reigning house" is all that Elgin feels, "an anach-
ronism of the heart" (58), which has no connection to actual Royals
who spend taxpayers' money. Elgin is much less concerned with
England than England would like to think: "The Government might
become the sole employer of labour in those islands, Church and
school might part company forever, landlords might be deprived
of all but compassionate allowances and, except for the degree of
extravagance involved in these propositions, they would hardly be
current in Elgin" (59). Elgin is not particularly interested in the
affairs of the Empire: "It was recognized dimly that England had
a foreign policy, more or less had to have it, as they would have
said in Elgin" (59). While these passages certainly point out the
narrow Elgin concentration on "the immediate, the vital, the municipal" (60), they also ironically denigrate the ethnocentric British
view that the citizens of the colonies must be interested in everything that happens "at home." In the novel, the British focus just
as vitally on "parish affairs" (125) as the citizens of Elgin; they are,
in their way, more provincial than the Canadians, as Lorne Murchison finds out: they are "more interested in the back garden fence
than anything else" (132). The British make the mistake of assuming that their interests and views are universal, at least throughout
the Empire; Duncan points out that in Elgin, the immediate issues
of "the town, the Province, the Dominion" (59) are, quite justifiably,
more important.

Duncan intimately links her deviation from the reader's political
and social expectations to her breaking of literary conventions in
order to express colonial reality. When Hugh and Advena are alone
in the library one evening, the narrator metaphorically waits in the
hall, trying to decide whether to break in on them or not. The
social convention of chaperonage (which Duncan takes as a serious
English custom in *Those Delightful Americans*) and the literary convention of the romantic tête-à-tête seem to demand that the narrator enter the library and witness the scene between Hugh and
Advena. But she takes the Elgin point of view on both conventions:
"It would simply have been considered, in Elgin, stupid to go into
the library" (88). The narrator concurs with Canadian social practice
and takes the reader into the dining room, where Lorne and his
parents are meeting with Lawyer Cruikshank. This clash of social
customs resulting from the narrator's defence of Elgin recurs
throughout the book; conventional narrative and the colonial point

of view meet to produce a distinctive form of narrative that represents Elgin.

Duncan's third-person narrators, as well as the first-person narrators who are characters in the novels, are often obtrusive in their attempts to create the background values of society in India and Canada. But Duncan's use of the omniscient narrator does not necessarily imply an incomplete understanding of the technique of realism. Dramatic method is not always suitable for the author writing, from the viewpoint of a colonial, about a colonial situation. The techniques of American realism depend on agreement between author and reader as to what reality is – a "common vision."[19] Duncan's viewpoint is by definition a minority one; she must carefully delineate the norms of the culture of which she writes so that the reader may clearly understand the point of view that the novel presents. The intrusive authorial voice so often found in Canadian novels has its basis in the colonial status of the authors, who feel that they must specify the social norms and recover the cultural context of their stories for readers totally unfamiliar with both the physical surroundings and the system of values prevalent in Canada.[20] The narrator of Duncan's novels must present the norms of a colonial society – norms that are often alien to readers – in order to present fully a colonial point of view.

Failure to correctly construct the colonial point of view, to read the irony, is demonstrated by Alfred Hesketh, the British visitor to Elgin in *The Imperialist*. The narrator provides a clear critique of Hesketh long before he arrives in Canada; the reader is prepared to decipher ironic jabs that the Canadians level at the ignorant "Britisher" and which he is totally unable to comprehend. Hesketh comes to Canada fully prepared to adapt to the different social customs, he feels, and congratulates himself on his reaction to the "initiation." However, despite his efforts, he makes social gaffes that prove his inability to locate the Canadian point of view. When he meets Alec Murchison in the family store, he ignores Alec's polite enquiries about his trip and, in a manner that he considers to be egalitarian, begins to ask about the sales of bicycles. Murchison replies that he sells more spoons than bicycles, pointing out to the alert reader the condition of Canadian roads, the nature of Elgin shoppers, and Alec's opinion of such useless fads. When Hesketh persists, Murchison suggests he purchase a bicycle at a rival store. Hesketh interprets the comment as an indication that Canada "must be an easy country to make money in" (153). Similarly, Hesketh has difficulty adapting to the Canadian use of the word "sir." He hears Lorne complain that, in England, working men have difficulty communicating their ideas because they feel obliged to present them with respectful "sirs": "They do 'sir' you a lot over there, don't they? ... It was as much as I could do to get at what a fellow of that sort meant, tumbling over the 'sirs' he propped it up with" (152). Hesketh misses the social implications of Lorne's comment, however, and interprets it as a transatlantic semantic quibble. When John Murchison later uses the colloquial expression "No sir!" (154), Hesketh ignores the changed social situation and displays his ignorance of Canadian social and linguistic idiom. He interprets Murchison's "sir" as a working man's deference to him as a British gentleman, and says "You won't use that form with me" (154).

In her account of Hesketh's speech at a rural election rally the narrator more seriously ridicules him for his ignorance of the Canadian point of view. Hesketh addresses the farmers of Fox County in support of Lorne Murchison's views on the Empire, but he is unaware of the social standards of his audience and seems unable to decipher their obvious distaste for his words. The farmers of Fox County are quite different from a British audience, the narrator explains in some detail, with "less stolid aggressiveness than their parallels in England, if they have parallels there." They are a new political breed, "democrats who had never thrown off the monarch," prosperous, but "not prosperous enough for theories and doctrines" (191). Hesketh's speech, larded with pompous quotations gleaned from various "noble lords" and filled with platitudes about colonial involvement in imperial wars, does not address the hard commercial facts of imperial union that his audience has uppermost in its mind. The farmers respond vigorously with their own concerns. While Hesketh trusts to "loftier principles than those of the marketplace" to regulate business, his audience is less trusting: "How be ye goin' to get 'em kept to, then?" a heckler calls out (194). The narrator relates that the audience "neglected the opportunity for applause" and Hesketh retires to the schoolroom's dunce seat, which, says the narrator, "had been used once before that day to isolate conspicuous stupidity" (195). The Englishman's inability to read irony allows the narrator and the reader to recognize him as an alien and themselves as part of a common community of intercultural interpreters.

The judgment is confirmed several days later when Hesketh is reminded of his failure. He encounters a child on the street who asks ironically, "Say mister, how's the dook?" (196). The comment invites the reader to fill in the Elgin assessment of Hesketh's political performance – the colonial perspective – in order to understand the significance of the child's remark. The phonetic spelling (dook), meant to represent Southern Ontario Americanized pronunciation, underlines the joke at his expense; he has not taken into account that Canada, while British, is North American as well. Hesketh is unable to read the colonial point of view because he is unable to see that it is different from his own.

THE NARRATORS of the Indian novels rely on a reader with knowledge of imperial-colonial relations between India and England and the accompanying popular literature of Anglo-India as well as sympathy for the colonial point of view. The works of Rudyard Kipling and other contemporary novelists offer an introduction to the Anglo-Indian colonial community that is the setting for many of Duncan's novels – a community haunted by memories of the Mutiny of 1857 in which the British were slaughtered by rioting soldiers. Consistently criticized by the British press and the opposition benches in Parliament, Anglo-Indians felt that they were not supported by the public they served in their attempt to bring the benefits of English culture to India.[21] Plagued by serious illness (often the result of some combination of corsets, pregnancy, poor sanitation, and heat) and engaged in almost daily cultural clashes with the Indian majority, the Anglo-Indian community was generally homesick, inward-looking, and resentful. In addition, the Anglo-Indian felt quite natural resentment toward the British voter who, despite the fact that he had never ventured further east than Dover, had the power to affect the laws administered in India and, indirectly, the physical safety of every "white" person in the country. Although Anglo-India represented the imperial power, Anglo-Indians felt that they were part of an overlooked, misunderstood colony.

The reader familiar with and sympathetic to this Anglo-Indian self-portrait would have the correct point of view for such ironical portraits as Miss Lavinia Moffat of *Vernon's Aunt*. Tausky suggests that the chief aim of the novel is "simple amusement";[22] however, the ironic depiction of Miss Moffat's naïveté is a serious comment upon interference by the British voter in questions of Indian government. Her genuine puzzlement over the Indian reluctance to discuss suttee and purdah with a strange Englishwoman on a train illustrates the causes of the Anglo-Indian resentment against know-nothing British interference and the "public opinion" fostered by fiction and the press. The ignorant parliamentary globetrotters who appear in Duncan's fiction become less figures of fun and more objects of serious alarm when one realizes, with the Anglo-Indian, that they have the power to materially affect the government of the country – more power, in fact, than the "old India hands" with whom they are contrasted.

The clash between the Anglo-Indian point of view and the know-nothing British is repeated in *The Simple Adventures of a Memsahib*. The plot involves the initiation of Helen Peachey into Anglo-Indian society as the wife of "young Browne," a member of an import-export firm in Calcutta. The story is told by Mrs Perth MacIntyre, wife of a senior partner in Browne's firm, whose selfconscious narrative includes references to the literary expectations of a British reader well versed in Kipling and the social expectations of a British visitor to Calcutta; she, however, is committed to the Anglo-Indian point of view, and looks forward to her own retirement to England with regret.

Helen Peachey and her British family (whose foibles perhaps stand in for the reader's own) are the initial victims of the narrator's irony. Their preparations for Helen's trip to Calcutta illustrate many of the typical British misapprehensions about India. Mrs Peachey, wife of an Anglican clergyman, imagines her daughter in a white dress "teaching a circle of little 'blacks' to read the Scriptures" (12). Helen's Aunt Plovtree "imparted an obscure idea of Helen's responsibility for the higher welfare of her domestics" (13) and imagines her learning Hindustani in the same way she learnt French and German in school. The females of the Peachey family have no standard by which to assess the contradictory advice they receive on the subject of Helen's trousseau; they are unaware that India has great variations in climate, and the fact that none of their retired Anglo-Indian advisers spent any time in Calcutta is a triviality that "escaped the attention of the Peachey family" (9). After the fuss of endless inquiries and maternal worries, Helen ends up with the trousseau that common sense would have dictated in the beginning: she is outfitted, "with the addition of a few muslin frocks ... almost exactly as if she were going to live in England" (9).

The preconceptions of British readers who innocently vote in favour of English-style social-reform measures for India are ridiculed in the narrator's attack on Mr Jonas Batcham, a Labour MP who stays with the Brownes while he investigates Indian society in his capacity as a representative of the people. Mr Batcham, "one of the largest manufacturers in the north of England" (170) (a self-characterization confirmed by his girth), has come to India chiefly, he states, to investigate the condition of the downtrodden workers in the jute and cotton mills – "the grinding of the faces of the poor, through our culpable neglect in failing to provide India with the humane limitations of a Factories Act" (179). The narrator points out the real reason why Batcham is solicitous about the health of the "factory-wallah": Batcham wants to enforce the British Factories Act in India – not out of sympathy for the poor, but in order to improve the competitive position of his own factory (179). The narrator explains in detail the Anglo-Indian view of the factories, which she says "accommodate themselves – not of philanthropy but of necessity – to the customs of the country" (181–2). When Batcham cannot find evidence of the mass exploitation of Indian factory workers, his Indian friends contrive to manufacture it for him by bribing his informants.

Batcham's speculations on the connection of ill-health and furloughs among Anglo-Indians are more serious. Concerned discussion of the health problems of several of Browne's friends and the sudden death of an "uncovenanted" (unpensioned) father of four young children prompt Batcham to the callous remark that the climate has done him nothing but good, and the prevalence of illness among Anglo-Indians is imagination. Mr Sayter, an "old India hand," replies acidly:

"I'm perfectly certain," said he, with a crispness in every syllable, "that Mr. Batcham has been benefited by staying six weeks in India. If he stayed six years he would doubtless be more benefited still. I daresay, as he says, we would all be benefited if it were not for our imaginations. It's a climate that leaves only one thing to be desired, and if some people say that's a coffin, that is clearly their imagination. Uncovenanted people have a way of dying pretty freely, but that's out of sheer perverseness to get more furlough. Most of them go for ever because they can't arrange it any other way. As for cholera, I give you my word not one man in ten dies of cholera out here; they go off with typhoid or dysentery, or in some comfortable way like that, and probably have a punka the whole time they're ill." (202–3)

The scene shows the danger of British gossip and hearsay about India. Sayter makes his point – those who have no commitment to the country have no right to criticize – just as the 9:30 PM gun sounds, reminding Batcham of the Mutiny. Sayter goes on: "'Oh, we'll have another Mutiny,' Mr Sayter remarked; 'it's quite on the cards. But you must not be alarmed, Mr. Batcham. It won't be,' he added irrepressibly, 'till after you go home'" (203).

THE GLIMPSES of everyday tragedy in the Anglo-Indian community that give *The Simple Adventures of a Memsahib* its tone of sadness and regret show that the narrator's sympathies are firmly with her colonial community, despite her understanding of imperial imperatives. The serious effects of the weather on health are only one aspect of Indian life for the English; simpler human sorrows also abound. The Brownes's wedding, organized by a new acquaintance, takes place far from Helen's family and friends. As Mrs Perth MacIntyre encounters the bride's bewildered face in the receiving line, she recalls that "all the people of the Rectory, who ought to have been at the wedding, were going about their ordinary business … Everybody who really cared was four thousand miles away, and unaware" (39). Although the narrator is aware of the various kinds of inflexibility that characterize the Anglo-Indian community, her irony is much gentler when directed at "insiders." As Mrs Perth MacIntyre reminds the reader: "I like the Brownes. They are nice young people" (306).

Duncan displays the same sympathetically defensive irony toward the Anglo-Indian community in *Set in Authority*. She characterizes as legitimate the indifference in the Calicut Club to British opinion on the Morgan case:

What they thought in London was a matter of great indifference in India. There they were thinking for themselves. When it came to a tea duty or a sugar bounty, attention was paid, however exasperated, to the home view; but in matters intrinsically Indian the home view was felt to be superfluous. Reuter duly cabled the opinions of the *Organ* and the *Remembrancer* as to the Indian Government's action in the Morgan case, and they said in the Calicut Club that it was sickening. From their point it *was* sickening; but as this is not a social study of an Anglo-Saxon group, isolated in a far country under tropical skies and special conditions, but only a story, I cannot stop to explain why ... The fact that they were politically equipped in no way whatever to deal with it only further heated their blood and intensified their conviction. (206)

As in *The Imperialist*, the British assumption that colonials care what the British think is challenged and ridiculed; and the colonial view is given legitimacy by the statement that, from their point of view, "it was sickening."

Duncan also uses irony based on the shared colonial experience of women to attack those who denigrate or stereotype women. In "A Mother In India,"[23] she considers the natural relationship of mother and daughter in both its stereotyped and its actual aspects. The unconventional mother, Helena, has gained an outsider's knowledge of the limiting stereotypes of women because she has been forced to adapt to colonial life. Having lived through the threat of fatal illness and plague, the intellectual desert of the isolated hill-station, the heat, and the constant mobility demanded by her husband's profession, Helena has little patience with the limiting role of mother that is thrust upon her by her reunion with her daughter. Cecily has grown up in a conventional English country home with her spinster aunts, wholly a part of the conventions that they represent and consciously embodying the modesty and feminine delicacy that her mother has discarded. For both, the reunion is a conscious confrontation between colonial reality and specifically English stereotypes of femininity.

Helena's narrative voice is the sympathetic voice of the colonial outsider. She recounts the story of the early years of her marriage when she and her husband lived on a strict budget in remote areas of India. The birth of the sickly Cecily to her nineteen-year-old mother precedes by one month her father's near-fatal brush with enteric fever. Helena must choose between the husband and the child, between a life identified with India or England. Cecily is sent to her father's family in England, and Helena remains. While Cecily grows up in a society that unquestioningly accepts the rightness of rural middle-class British manners, of "pussies and vicars and elderly ladies" (10), Helena identifies with "the look of wider seas and skies, the casual experienced glance, the touch of irony and of tolerance" of the Anglo-Indians – as she says, "My own people" (9–10).

When Cecily is twenty-one, the two are reunited for Cecily's trip to India to join her parents. The active, ironic Helena very quickly perceives that she has little in common with her English-bred daughter, and she has even less in common with the "maternal virtues" that are part of the stereotype of "mother" which her daughter and her friends expect her to assume: "I put them on with care every morning and wore them with patience all day" (21). Dacres Tottenham, her male friend, reimposes the patriarchal definition of the feminine upon Helena as soon as he discovers that she is, in fact, a mother. He insists that there must be a biological sympathy between them, and finds Helena's distance from Cecily unwomanly:

"Don't you find yourself in sympathy with her?" he asked.

"My dear boy, I have seen her just twice in twenty-one years! You see, I've always stuck to John."

"But between mother and daughter – I may be old-fashioned, but I had an idea there was an instinct that might be depended on." (13)

Dacres insists that the relation between mother and daughter is "a beatitude" (14) and condemns Helena as an unnatural mother. Helena likens his imposition of a stereotyped definition upon her to the infallible authority of the Catholic Church: "The primitive man in him rose up as Pope of nature and excommunicated me as a creature recusant to her functions" (18). Dacres claims the authority to determine who is a woman, and Helena does not quite measure up.

Dacres's sympathy for Cecily is born of his anger at Helena's refusal to counterfeit the maternal role, but rapidly turns into a desire to marry Cecily because she fits his idea of femininity. Dacres accepts the simple stereotype of feminine passivity and nurturance, and his desire to marry Cecily in order to have a natural resting place for his volatile nature is the object of the irony shared by reader and narrator. For Dacres, "simple elemental goodness" and "domestic virtues" (25) are the essence of woman: "She is a girl Ruskin would have loved" (22), he argues, recalling Ruskin's notoriously limiting description of women's nature and social role in "Of Queen's Gardens." Dacres mistakes Cecily's dull blockishness for simplicity and directness. The narrator remarks that "men are very slow in changing their philosophy about women" (14); Dacres's philosophy seems to have more effect on his view of Helena and Cecily than does reality.

The reader accepts Helena's judgment that, in general, Cecily "could see no more than the bulk, no further than the perspective; she could register exactly as much as a camera" (31). Dacres finally recognizes Cecily's dullness when she objects to viewing the Taj Mahal by moonlight because of the dampness of the dew. But the negative judgment recoils on Helena, whose comments on Dacres's love for Cecily were motivated in part by her resentment of the maternal role and jealousy of Cecily's ability to fascinate Dacres. She must endure a lifetime of Cecily's intrusive good intentions because Cecily refuses all her suitors, claiming that no one less interesting than Dacres could ever hold her love. Helena learns that even Cecily does not completely fit the patriarchal stereotype of a sweet, brainless woman.

The limiting stereotypes of woman's role that the colonial Helena has sloughed off are explicitly related to the simple British manners of Cecily's middle-class upbringing; the story thus reveals an additional dimension of meaning in the clash of the colony and the centre. Britain can respond to the unconventionality, the volatility bred in colonial life, just as Cecily can and will respond to such colonial values in Dacres; the colonial is unjustified in too quickly condemning the British conventionality that seems to pass an unfavourable judgment on the rough life of the colony. Both sides in the colonial-imperial dialogue are capable of responding to each other, and yet they are unaware of that capability.

Duncan's narrators offer a model for reading irony; the reader must attempt to assume the ironist's point of view, to find the positive values, as James puts it, that lie behind the ironic ones. The controlled, limited irony directed against representatives of imperial powers in Duncan's work is decipherable against the background of the positive values that it implies. It is also radically political, serving to consolidate cultural groups by encouraging readers to recognize the values that they share with other members and creating a subversive portrait of the imperial who is ignorant of the everyday life of a colonial. Thus the creation of the colonial point of view is sanctioned by the novels themselves; they invite the participation of the reader who, by applying both the public knowledge invoked by the narrators and the private knowledge of life as a woman and a colonial, deciphers the irony, gets the joke, and is enabled to "come to just conclusions upon very slight data."

CHAPTER THREE

Idealism, Realism, and Literary Convention: "Truth of One Sort or Another"

Sara Jeannette Duncan is often considered one of the first significant advocates of literary realism in Canada. Desmond Pacey finds her among "the few defenders of the new realism"[1] in late-nineteenth-century Canada, and T.D. MacLulich discusses *The Imperialist* as an "early example of a full-realised realistic novel."[2] Duncan began writing reviews and novels during the "realism war" waged by William Dean Howells and his supporters in British and American periodicals, and her comments on Howells in *The Week* and the *Montreal Star* seem to lend support to the realist side. Yet Duncan's readers note a certain ambivalence in the attitude to realism demonstrated in her novels. Thomas Tausky suggests that Duncan merely attempts to avoid the extremes of the controversy by utilizing both styles in her work, and finds that "elements of realism and romance co-exist, sometimes happily, sometimes uneasily, in her novels."[3] Marian Fowler similarly finds a "divided allegiance"[4] to both realism and romance in Duncan's work. Both critics imply that Duncan was somehow too psychologically defensive to fully understand realism, but many of Duncan's statements suggest that the mix of realism and romance in her work is a conscious decision to write against the exclusively materialist world-view she associated with Howells and his style of realism. While Duncan agreed with the realists that literature must reflect observed reality, she included as part of that reality transcendent values often associated with romance.

Duncan's seemingly contradictory statements about realistic techniques have puzzled critics. Tausky attributes her mix of realistic and romantic ideas to her "patriotic desire to see Canadian literature flourish, and an awareness of higher standards else-where."[5] Canadian writing at the time was predominantly romantic, according to Tausky, and so of a standard lower on a modern scale than the US realistic writing that Duncan admired; in her reviews of Canadian works, Tausky suggests, she was torn between her loyalty to her compatriots and her own desire for excellence. This analysis seems especially appropriate in the case that he cites – Duncan's review of *The Algonquin Maiden*, a novel by two of her fellow journalists at *The Week*. She praises the factual basis of the novel yet also defends the romantic excesses of the plot against those who would make realism the only basis for evaluation. Duncan scorns those who worship the "commonplace," yet, as Tausky points out, she seems to do the same thing in her own novels. He concludes that, while she attempted to throw off the old assumptions of Victorian culture in her defence of realism, she could not yet understand "the drift towards a modern consciousness" that a full acceptance of realism would imply; instead, she remained "divided in her loyalties," psychologically unable to completely throw off Victorian romance and yet yearning toward modernism.[6]

Fowler amplifies Tausky's assessment of Duncan's ambivalence towards modern realism. She sees Duncan's career as a gradual fall from the tough-minded realism of the early books to the sentimental romance of the later ones. While working as a journalist – "in actual practice writing realistically," Fowler writes – Duncan was, in theory, siding with romance and so "leaving the door open for herself later in her career." Her attachment to realism was a necessary part of her attachment to her "new father-figure" Howells, though her work continued to show "divided loyalties": "In her writing, she vacillated from realism to romance, and the latter, as time passed, tended to surface in her fiction in awkward and pathetic little fantasy leaps."[7] This view of Duncan's realism is of a piece with Fowler's general treatment of Duncan as a neurotic and unfulfilled woman desperately trying to smooth over the insufficiencies of her own life with exotic fictions. Fowler seems to argue that Duncan's personality prevented her from having a coherent approach to realism.

Many of the seeming inconsistencies in Duncan's view of realism are resolved, however, when her statements are taken in their context of nineteenth-century Canadian idealism. Duncan believed that "realities" and "idealities" could be resolved within a framework that insisted upon the relationship between the real and the ideal. She salvaged the romantic "idealities" that Canadians derived from their literary dialogue with Victorian poetry even while she wrote within the growing dominance of materialist realism, writing against the assumption that only those things that can be explained by physical cause and effect are real. Even in her most realistic writing she applied her theory, connecting realistic detail with the ideal it represents by creating typical, representative characters and by both acknowledging and challenging the "ideal" structures of narrative that conventionally represent reality.

DUNCAN'S INTEREST in realism was prompted in part by her admiration of the works of Howells and Henry James,[8] but realism in Canada was not a wholly foreign idea. Many of the factors that led to the growth of realism in American fiction were also present in Canada, and so Canadian realism can be thought of as taking a parallel rather than an imitative course. Critics in nineteenth-century Canadian magazines insisted upon realism as a moral antidote to the deleterious effects of romantic fiction. W.P.C., writing in *The Literary Garland* in 1848, despaired of the "insipid nonsense" and "polluting licentiousness" of romantic fiction and called for a more practical literature that focused on the material "that nature has furnished ready to our hand."[9] The sketches of Thomas Chandler Haliburton and Thomas McCulloch emphasized realistic detail in the tradition of the eighteenth-century moral essay, whose final test of value was an appeal to nature. McCulloch offers a spirited defence of realism in his *Letters of Mephibosheth Stepsure* when his narrator is criticized by "Censor" for including details of Nova Scotia life that are "offensive to decency." Censor finds the language of the letters too realistic: "The fancy of the writer in no case transports him to Parnassus to pluck a single flower which adorns and scents that delightful mountain ... Both the Muses and the Graces would pronounce their ban on the letters; the first for the insipidity and coldness of the composition, the last for the offences against delicacy with which they are interspersed." McCulloch replies with a sketch depicting his narrator and his rustic friends transported to Parnassus to pluck the flowers, which ends as Censor tumbles off the peak and lands in a pile of dung left by his trusty mount Pegasus. Concerning his letters, the narrator avers, "I never sell my potatoes for flowers" and states that his literary task is to "leave bombast and doggerel, and gather common sense."[10] McCulloch's point, that the language must suit the subject matter, is one often made by eighteenth-century writers; it is given extra force by the manifest absurdity of applying Censor's Old-World language to the differing reality of the New World.

Howells's comments in "The Editor's Study" show that US realism was also supported by the protestant dislike of romantic fiction. In his column for April 1887, Howells replies to a letter that taxes fiction with begetting such "high-strung and supersensitive ideas of life that plain industry and plodding perseverance are despised."[11] Howells defends fiction by agreeing that the "unmoral romance" is injurious to spiritual health: "The whole spawn of so-called unmoral romances, which imagine a world where the sins of sense are unvisited by the penalties following, swift or slow, but inexorably sure, in the real world, are deadly poison: these do kill," (99). He argues that fiction that is true to "the motives, the impulses, the principles that shape the life of actual men and women" is necessarily "full of divine and natural beauty" (101). Like the Canadians, he refers to eighteenth-century models to justify his theory, citing Edmund Burke to justify his claim that truth to nature is the only test for literature.

Canadian realists began to take their own way in the war of realism and romance in the Confederation era. They insisted that, while stereotyped characters and stock references to the ideal must be expunged from New-World literature in favour of a reflection of the actual conditions of life, fiction is more than a simple mirror image. Like Duncan, many Canadian authors believed that there is no essential contradiction between realism as a literary technique and idealism as an ideological base for fiction, and that the best fiction makes use of both. In "A Note On Russian Realism," Charles G.D. Roberts argues that Russian realistic works prove that realism and idealism are necessary components of all great fiction: "If we had never been forced to make acquaintance with any other realism than this of the Russian Masters, there would have been no question at issue between realism and idealism. It would have been a patent truth that the two are inseparable in all work of the highest, and that the sanity, the symmetry, the applicability, of ideal creations are secured by dependence upon a selective realism." Roberts advocates the use of the ideal to guide the selection of realistic detail. He approves of Nikolay Gogol, because in his work "we are struck by an abundance of detail; but it is such detail only as tells appreciably toward the desired effect."[12] He finds French works unrealistic because they focus on the lowest elements of human nature and ignore the highest aspirations of men. Without specifying authors, he finds US realists dull and commercial.[13]

Early twentieth-century writers in Canada espoused a theory of realistic writing that connected the specific detail of lifelike description to a higher or transcendent life. In his article "Fiction and Reality," Stephen Leacock concludes a lengthy defence of the fictional method of Charles Dickens with a statement of this theory of fiction: "But we understood him to say that the truth was that from the time of the Romans onward Art had of necessity proceeded by the method of selected particulars and conspicuous qualities; that this was the nature and meaning of art itself ... that by this means and this means only could the real truth – the reality greater than life be portrayed."[14] Frederick Philip Grove refers to the importance of "that soul which is common to us all" in the creation of fiction, which he characterizes as "the almost mystical fusing of the two things which are needed – a thing presented and a soul presenting." He argues that those who focus on scientific accuracy offer a spiritually impoverished view of life, and, in contrast, the "realist" pares away circumstantial detail in order to reach a kind of mythic truth.[15] Duncan might then be seen as part of a tradition in Canadian prose and fiction that rejected a narrow materialist focus in favour of the inclusion of some form of transcendent reality in realistic work.

In *The Meaning of Contemporary Realism*, George Lukacs differentiates between two types of realism: "modernist realism" based on a belief in the primacy of the subjective and the impossibility of meaningful contact with objective reality, and "bourgeois critical realism" which views man as an element in a progressive historical reality, individuated in relation to it and capable of influencing it. While Lukacs is discussing fiction written mainly since the First World War, his categories have some relevance when considering Duncan and her contemporaries. Howells was not a modernist writer, for he maintained that the individual could act; however, his destruction of an ideal of absolute value led the way towards the chaotic subjectivity of William Faulkner and the later twentieth-

century writers and towards the fiction of the American "progressive movement." Duncan's defence of the traditional "bourgeois
critical realist" novel represents a rejection of modernist ideology
at its roots. She is thus one of a group of anti-modernist Canadian
writers who continue to refer to ideals of absolute value not through
nostalgia or muddle-headedness but as part of a conscious rejection
of the narrow materialist vision that modernist realism implies.

Duncan's theory of literary realism is governed by her general
approach to art, which partakes of the idealism introduced to English literature by Thomas Carlyle and reinterpreted for Canada by
thinkers such as John Watson. Duncan insists upon the ideal as a
principle for selecting artistic detail; the human soul is the means
whereby the artist links the multitude of physical sensations
received by the individual to the ideals that they represent in the
concrete world. Like Roberts, her contemporary, she puts equal
weight on the real and the ideal, and in the process of relating the
two she finds a pattern for social reform.

   Duncan's realism is based in the particular form of idealism that
she encountered in the writings of Carlyle and Matthew Arnold.[16]
In Carlyle's *Sartor Resartus*, the fictitious idealist philosopher Herr
Teufelsdrock enunciates concisely the central idealist tenet that the
external world is an incomplete embodiment of eternal ideas: "All
visible things are emblems; what thou seest is not there on its own
account; strictly taken, is not there at all; Matter exists only spiritually, and to represent some Idea, and body it forth."[17] Duncan
makes the idealist view of the world into a principle of selection
for her novels; realistic detail must not be included in and for itself
but must refer the reader to the "idea" that it represents. Duncan
illustrates the use of realistic detail to refer to an idea in her description of an organ-grinder's monkey in *The Week*: "I prize him as one
of the few picturesque incidents in our over-practical civilization.
There is nothing idyllic about the organ-grinder, but there is about
the idea which he embodies. How soon, I wonder, shall we have
a municipal enactment forbidding the purveying of popular airs
unless expressly contracted for?"[18] The organ-grinder embodies the
idea of popular music freely enjoyed – a rebellion against the
increasingly materialist and wholly practical arrangements of the
modern city. That idea constitutes a good; Duncan does not specify

whether she identifies it with Plato's ideas, God, Arnold's moral absolute, or any other idealist system. The context of the novels suggests a system of ideals based in the traditions of British history, but the system is never specifically defined; Duncan seems to take for granted a similar veneration of vague "idealities" in the sympathetic reader.[19]

Duncan's description of the Elgin market in *The Imperialist* is often cited as an example of her realistic technique, but close analysis reveals that the realistic description is tied specifically to an abstract idea that serves to unite Lorne with his countrymen. The idea that connects Lorne to the farmers of Fox County is "opportunity," a quality that Duncan describes in her journalism as the central idea of North America.[20] At an early turning point in his life, Lorne realizes that, like the farmers who sit in the market in Elgin, he too can find the opportunity to make his mark in the comparative emptiness and newness of the new land. The piles of hay and cordwood, "fruit, vegetables and poultry" presided over by wives "with their knees drawn up and their skirts tucked close, vigilant in rusty bonnets" are described minutely, but not for their own sake – they represent "the narrow inheritance of opportunity to live which generations had grasped before" (73). Lorne, who has just been given sole charge of an important legal case, also feels the sense of opportunity "which, if he could seize and hold, would lift and carry him on" (74). This "great piece of luck," opportunity in the abstract, allows him to see to the heart of what the farmers represent: "The sense of kinship surged in his heart; these were his people, this his lot as well as theirs. For the first time he saw it in detachment. Till now he had regarded it with the friendly eyes of a participator who looked no further. Today he did look further"(74). What Lorne is enabled to see is not simply the farmers but "the idea they represented, which had become for him suddenly moving and pictorial." Through "imagination and energy and love," he is able to understand the transcendent reality that the actual world represents, "moving and pictorial" (74). Lorne becomes a kind of Canadian Carlylean hero, able to see through the realities of this world into the idealities that they represent.[21]

The entire novel is governed by a similar tension between "a romantic world of imagination and controlling world of hard fact." The expectations and practicalities of the Elgin townspeople are always "bringing the imagination back to earth, containing and disciplining it";[22] Lorne's weakness (and the weakness of the social reformer John Church in *His Honor and a Lady*) is an inability to adequately take reality into account when he attempts to reform the world according to his ideal vision. The imagination is not ultimately defeated in *The Imperialist*, however; Advena and Hugh are taught how to bring their romantic dreams of renunciation into line with Canadian reality, and, though Lorne learns the hard lesson of political defeat, he still "goes forth to his share in the task" of nation building (268).

Duncan's statements on the theory of realism generally support the principle of the ideal as a selective tool in realistic fiction. In *The Week* she defends the realistic novel against a critic who asserts that realism is simply a slice of life, "requiring only a concentration of one's attention upon the details of one's neighbours' daily life, an accurate transcription thereof, and a great deal of assurance." Duncan rejects the view that realism simply copies life and says instead that realism is a selective art, involving "the connecting of each of these trivial, common actions" to "the complex ethical structure of human nature."[23] She criticizes journalists "to whom no episode is too unimportant, no incident too revolting"[24] for inclusion in news stories; she ironically portrays the problems inherent in balancing realistic description with artistic aim in her account of a vacation cruise along the shores of Lake Ontario, in company with "some half-dozen bags of an agricultural product, the lumpy and uninteresting nature of which will never be made public through the medium of this pen."[25] The description of a commonplace scene or detail must not exist in and for itself but must point to a larger idea.

Duncan's theory of the necessity of realistic detail to point to ideal reality suggests a kind of allegorical method in her creation of characters. Like James, she chooses detail "to be typical, to be inclusive"[26] and so creates characters who are illustrative of groups and of complexes of ideas. Duncan's use of such representative characters to depict social ideas in *The Imperialist* has been remarked upon by Claude Bissell, who suggests a symbolic function for the two love stories in the novel. The final triumph of Advena's love for Hugh Finlay, Bissell suggests, represents Duncan's view that Old-World honour must bow to Canadian judgments in Canada; the demise of Lorne's attachment for the anglophilic Dora Milburn parallels his disillusionment with imperialism. However, as Bissell rightly remarks, "All this is achieved by the novelist through the implications of her human drama";[27] Duncan offers little in the way of direct statement, although the implications of her "drama" are clear. J.M. Zezulka also comments that "what the characters represent is at least as important as who or what they are." He finds "an almost allegorical infrastructure which breaks the surface in the novel's concluding paragraph, where Lorne's partnership with Cruikshank provides us with an explicit analogy for Canada's participation in the Imperial Scheme."[28]

The names of Duncan's characters often indicate their representative function. Graham Trent, the hero of *Cousin Cinderella*, in some senses represents the heroic virtues of his country,[29] and he is named for a major river system in his native land.[30] The morally admirable but rather inflexible hero of *His Honor, and a Lady* is John Church; the civil-servant hero of *The Burnt Offering*, John Game, keeps up a losing battle for stability and progress in the Indian government. Prince Alfred in *His Royal Happiness* is destined to reunite the Anglo-Saxon race on the eve of the First World War through a treaty with the us; his name and his nickname, "Cakes," recall the legendary King Alfred who united his countrymen to drive out European invaders.[31] As the narrator tells us in *The Imperialist*, "We must take this matter of names seriously" (17).

The narrators of Duncan's novels often directly suggest representative functions for the characters as well. When Alfred Hesketh arrived in Elgin he "stood for a symbol as well as for a stranger" (*Imp.*, 151). Mrs Crow is not simply a realistic farm wife; she is also "the sum of a certain measure of opportunity and service" (*Imp.*, 188). In *The Burnt Offering*, Ganendra Thakore "stands for the soul of the people" (147) of India, and the effect of his trial speech on his Indian audience confirms this status, while British MP Vulcan Mills "stood for [the] actual and private emotions" (12) of his constituents in Further Angus.

Elfrida Bell and Janet Cardiff, the two writers who figure as main characters in *A Daughter of Today*, discuss this process of creating characters as representative types. Elfrida defends the French *roman psychologique* – which found its subject matter in the "scientific" portrayal of illegitimacy, prostitution, alcoholism, and murder – against more conventional work by Howells that aims to portray the whole of society. Janet speaks more reasonably of the sincerity of Howells's tone, and she implies that the British or American

writer is not justified in using sensational subject matter because
it is not typical of British or American society: "But do you know
I don't think the English or American people are exactly calculated
to offer the sort of material you mean. The *bête* is too conscious
of his moral fibre when he's respectable; and when he isn't respectable he doesn't commit picturesque crimes – he steals and boozes"
(114). Elfrida objects, citing the case of Wainwright, a minor art
critic turned forger and poisoner, whose life furnished material for
Bulwer Lytton, Dickens, and Oscar Wilde. Janet points out that
Wainwright was an exception to the rule and so not fair game for
the serious artist. True art proceeds according to representative
types and typical examples, she argues: "He illustrates my case;
amongst us he was a phenomenon, like the elephant-headed man.
Phenomena are for the scientists. You don't mean to tell me that
any fiction that pretends to call itself artistic has any right to touch
them? ... We're a conventional people ... And so are you, for how
could you change your spots in a hundred years?" (115). Janet
opposes ideal art to mere sensationalism; Elfrida opposes stale
conventionality to fresh observation of the individual case. The
story seems to imply that both are partially right – Elfrida's novel
is published by the same firm as Janet's, and both are successful.[32]

ALTHOUGH HOWELLS'S INFLUENCE on Duncan was undoubtedly
great,[33] in her journalism Duncan generally defines her own views
on realism in opposition to his statements. In a column for the
Montreal Star, she reacts to Howells's famous parable of the two
grasshoppers, in which he rejects any notion of the ideal.[34] Howells
comes close to denying that ideals are possible: "Possibly there is
no absolutely ugly, no absolutely beautiful."[35] Over Keats's line "A
thing of beauty is a joy forever," Howells chooses "Beauty is truth,
truth beauty" as his creed, and approvingly quotes Burke as part
of his argument that the only legitimate test of literature is its
fidelity to nature. He rejects the view that art defines itself in
relation to other art in his parable of two grasshoppers, one real,
and one ideal "made up of wire and cardboard, very prettily painted
in a conventional tint" which has "served to represent the notion
of a grasshopper ever since man emerged from barbarism ... We
hope the time is coming when not only the artist, but the common,
average man, who always 'has the standard of the arts in his power,'

will have also the courage to apply it, and will reject the ideal grasshopper wherever he finds it, in science, in literature, in art ... because it is not like a real grasshopper."[36] Duncan clearly understands Howells's point, but she wishes to modify it. She responds by again asserting the value of the ideal as a selective principle in fiction. She rejects Howells's implication that the novel must be true *either* to art *or* to nature, and says that the novel must be true to *both*: "Mr. Howells would probably kindly say to this that the measure of the art is the measure of its truth, and that there may be found the conclusion of the whole matter. Yet, it might be urged that the selective principle is surely not unimportant among the artist's brain tools, and that to neglect its use is to fail to be true to art."[37] The attention we pay to realistic detail in art is not, Duncan says, prompted by the worthiness of the thing depicted but by the art with which it is depicted. "A cabbage is a very essential vegetable to certain salads, but we do not prostrate ourselves adoringly before the cabbage in everyday life, and it is a little puzzling to know why we should be required to do so in art galleries and book stores, however perfect the representations there of cabbages, vegetable or human. If we do it is certainly purely the art which we admire, not the nature."[38] Duncan rejects Howells's artificial grasshopper because it is not lifelike, not because it is ideal. The types chosen by authors, she implies, must have some relation to the real as well as to the ideal.

In an earlier essay in *The Week*, Duncan considers the "disquietude in critical circles" caused by the friction between the new realism and the more traditional approach to literature. Following the practice of writers in *The Week*, Duncan styles the conflict a political one between "literary democracy" and authority, and she reconciles the two in an idealist vision of eternal verities embodied in a changing world. Duncan states that the "self-governing spirit of the age has invaded letters" in the works of Walt Whitman and other writers who question "why they, of all people, should be governed by crowned skeletons, and owe such strict allegiance to the sceptered hands of Westminster Abbey." The spirit of self-government in literature is opposed, Duncan writes, by a "strong faction for authority" including Arnold, James Russell Lowell, and John Ruskin. While the democratic group appeals to truth as the only measure of a work of art, the authority group depends upon comparison with the classics as canonized by British criticism.

Duncan reconciles the two warring factions by proposing that literature is a growth through which fundamental literary principles remain the same, but external manifestations alter: "In literature, as elsewhere, certain fundamental principles do not change. We must have truth of one sort or another – truth to certain values in the ideal, truth to certain actualities in the real. But, while its informing spirit must conform to these principles always, the body of literature is a growth – and growth itself means change."[39] Duncan's view of truth is significantly different from the view she ascribes to both the literary democrats and the authoritarians; she puts equal weight on truth to ideal values and truth to actual life. The informing spirit of literature must conform to the principles of the real and the ideal, even while its images change through growth and through the different growing conditions of the new world.

Duncan insists on the maintenance of a balance between the real and the ideal in contemporary fiction. She complains that too many writers focus on physical facts to the detriment of ideal values: "The modern school of fiction, if it is fairly subject to any reproach, may bear the blame of dealing too exclusively in the corporealities of human life, to the utter and scornful neglect of its idealities."[40] In her review of *The Algonquin Maiden*, by Ethelwyn Wetherald and Graeme Mercer Adam, she continues her criticism of realists who, she believes, attempt to make all novelists contract their horizons to mere physicality. While she approves of the attempt to describe that reality which "springs all around us, vital and fragrant, and flowering," she feels that literature should be more than "one long deification of the commonplace ... Gentlemen of the realistic school, one is disposed to consider you very right in so far as you go, but to believe you mistaken in your idea that you go the whole distance and can persuade the whole novel-writing fraternity to take the same path through the burdocks and the briars. Failing this, you evidently believe that you can put to the edge of the sword every wretched romancist who presumes to admire the exotic of the ideal, and to publish his admiration." Nonetheless, Duncan believes that even a romance must be based on fact. She criticizes the stylistic excesses (which she perhaps unjustly attributes to Ethelwyn Wetherald) as improbable and sometimes ludicrous. The word "maidens" has become "the exclusive property of Lord Tennyson" she protests, and is inappropriate anywhere else; a believable Algonquin chief would not speak of "writhing wreaths of thunderclouds descended to earth," she complains. She wishes that the "guiding and restraining hand" of Graeme Mercer Adam, who she says furnished the political and social basis for the story, "were evident upon more pages of *The Algonquin Maiden* than it is."[41]

Duncan's statements in her journalism that realism must take account of the "idealities" of life go some way towards explaining the inconsistency of narrative tone in *The Imperialist* identified by Peter Allen.[42] To his example of Duncan's deviations from the "general tone of sophisticated social comedy" in the interests of "unrestrained melodrama" might be added several other examples of romance narrative techniques intruding upon realistic plot and character: Betty Allen's prince and beggar-maid love story in the materialistic *The Gold Cure*, or the coincidental appearance of roses at strategic points in the love stories in *Cousin Cinderella* and *His Royal Happiness*. Whether or not such inconsistencies between serious social comedy and romance cliché "constitute a serious flaw"[43] to the modern critical mind, in the context of Duncan's stated opinions it is difficult to believe that this strategy is unconscious, as Allen seems to imply; Duncan clearly states in her journalism that both elements must be included in order to create good fiction.

THE NECESSITY of connecting the ideal with the real, and of preserving the ideal against the incursions of the real, is a prominent theme in all of Duncan's work. The Empire is a repository of ideal values that must be preserved against the materialist self-interest of individuals and nations in *An American Girl In London*, *The Imperialist*, *The Burnt Offering*, *His Royal Happiness*, *Set In Authority*, *His Honor, and a Lady*, and all of the wartime plays. The opposition between marriage for material reasons and for ideal reasons is the focus of love stories in *The Burnt Offering*, *The Gold Cure*, and *Title Clear*. The struggle between a materialist, utilitarian vision that is finally divisive, antagonistic, and selfish and one that is touched by imagination, insight, amelioration, and the man who lifts up his heart (as Duncan says of Lorne Murchison) is consistently dramatized in the novels, with a distinctly favourable judgment given to those who can join the two important elements of moral life into constructive action. The mission of Duncan's art, in both technique and theme, is to prevent a future characterized by the poverty of the merely material such as that of Vulcan Mills and his daughter Joan, of Judith Church before her marriage and emigration to India, of Mr Chafe and Mr Milburn.

Art and its ability to join the material and the ideal is the focus of Duncan's two extended treatments of the nature of the artist: *A Daughter of Today* and *The Path of a Star*. Elfrida Bell remains unable to create serious, successful art throughout *A Daughter of Today*, and part of her problem seems to be her inability to appropriately link the ideal and the real. In the scheme of nineteenth-century popular idealism, the transcendence of self is a necessary initial step toward the ability to see clearly both physical and transcendent reality. While the individual is bound up in self, the world seems only a series of physical sensations; the individual must transcend the stage of naive egotism to see common humanity. But, as Elfrida constantly reminds us, she is simply and wholly an egotist. She tells John Kendall, "My egotism is like a little flame within me. All the best things feed it, and it is so clear that I can see everything in its light" (126). Because she is so absorbed in self, she is unable to link reality and theory. When she is close to starving, she romanticizes her plight; she ignores her feelings for Kendall and declares that love is merely a physical urge (158).

The only fully realized piece of art in the novel is Kendall's portrait of Elfrida. Kendall recognizes it as "his consummate picture" (260), and Elfrida, whose powers of artistic observation are emphasized, declares it his best work. The power of the superior work of art is its ability to be true to both the real appearance of Elfrida and to Kendall's conception of her as an abstract idea. Kendall uses his extraordinary ability to reproduce the realistic look of things to express something that is beyond mere surfaces: "He had for once escaped ... the tyranny of his brilliant technique. He had subjected it to his idea, which had grown upon the canvas obscure to him under his own brush until that final moment; and he recognized with astonishment how relative and incidental the truth of the treatment seemed in comparison with the truth of the idea" (260).

Just before her death, Elfrida sends a note to Janet Cardiff to congratulate her on her engagement to Kendall. Elfrida blames Janet for not being totally candid about her relationship with Kendall, but again reveals her confusion over the relation between the real world and the ideal one. She had created an ideal of friendship, a "fair imagining" (268) that she blames Janet for not sharing: "I find you adulterating what ought to be the pure stream of ideality with muddy considerations of what people are pleased to call the moralities, and with the feebler contamination of the convention-alities"(267–8). Elfrida created her ideal of Janet out of nothing; when that ideal does not correspond to the real she is confused and unhappy. In the same letter she sends Janet a token that represents for her the idea of art – a token two stages removed from reality – a photograph of a painting.

The Path of a Star offers another discussion of the nature of the artist, and confirms the importance of realizing the ideal in real life. The novel focuses on the actress Hilda Howe and her love for Stephen Arnold, an Anglican priest sworn to celibacy. A parallel love story between the Salvation Army missionary Laura Filbert and Hilda's businessman friend Duff Lindsay shows the effect of a mistaken ideal in life.

Arnold is originally drawn to Hilda by her ability to dramatize the ideal for her audience, especially in her performance as Mary Magdalene in a biblical drama: "She did so much more than 'lift' the inventive vulgarisation of the Bible story in the common sense; she inspired and transfused it ... in his exultation he saw what it was to perform miracles, to remit sins. The spark of divinity that was in him glowed to a white heat; the woman on the stage warmed her hands at it in two consciousnesses" (67–9). Arnold had origi-nally detected in himself, "disguised with a host of spiritual wrap-pings" (26), a love of the artistic ideal, but he sublimated this love to his religious vows. Hilda brings this ideal to life again, and relates it directly to his religious life in her portrayal of Mary. Before he meets Hilda, he views himself as part of an abstract force, "a spiritual molecule rightly inspired and moving to the great future ... of the universal Kingdom" (26). Hilda similarly has the qualities of an unbodied soul, "expressing the ideals of the stage" (233) without settled social rank, and with a quality of personal plasticity that allows her to take on the attributes of any character. Arnold doubts the possibility of retaining the ideal in real life. In another context, he laments the diversion of religious enthusiasm into sec-ular life: "It's seeing another ideal pulled down, gone under, some-thing that held, as best it could, a ray from the source. It's another glimpse of the strength of the tide – terrible. It's a cruel hint that one lives above it in the heaven of one's own hopes, by some mere blind accident" (138). Arnold is discussing the possibility of Laura's marriage to Lindsay, but his comments reflect on his own relationship with Hilda. He continues to doubt the motives for their mutual attraction, and for a time they connect only through a kind of spiritual communication that Duncan seems to think is entirely possible, though not completely satisfactory. During Hilda's declaration of love, they reach a new level of spiritual intimacy: "Without a word a great tenderness of understanding filled the space between them; an interpreting compassion went to and fro. Suddenly a new light dawned in Hilda's eyes, she leaned forward and met his in an absorption which caught them out of themselves into some space where souls wander, and perhaps embrace. It was a frail adventure upon a gaze, but it carried them infinitely far" (227). The realization of a "spiritual sympathy" between them convinces Hilda that "all her desire for a lesser thing from him must creep away abashed forever" (229). Of course, her belief that their relationship can remain spiritual does not persist, but "even when the lesser thing, by infinitely gradual expansion, again became the greater, it remained permanently leavened and lifted in her by the strange and lovely incident that had taken for the moment such command of her and of him" (229). Arnold finally acknowledges his sexual love for Hilda, but this revelation does not secularize their ideal: "He trusted the new wings of his mortal love to bear his soul to its immortality" (309).

Duff Lindsay's love for Laura Filbert stands as a kind of parodic counterpoint to Hilda's romance. A dedicated captain in the Salvation Army, Laura is clearly more interested in souls than in money, which puts her above her fellow Salvationists. But Lindsay does not participate in her ideal; in fact, he does not at any point lift himself out of the materialist fantasy of how Laura will look in her new drawing room. Laura is inevitably drawn into his world and loses her ethereal religious charm. Lindsay reflects on his changed perspective while sitting with Hilda on the Maidan, and the sunset echoes his feelings about Laura: "As they sat without speaking, the heart of the after-glow drew away across the river, and left something chill and empty in the spaces about them. Things grew hard of outline, the Maidan became an unlimited expanse of commonplace, grey and unyielding; the lines of gas-lamps on the roads came very near. 'What a difference it makes!' Lindsay exclaimed, looking after the vanished light, 'and how suddenly it goes!'" (187). As the light of the ideal goes out of Laura, Lindsay notices that her neck is long and she has no chin. Laura's figure shows so many faults when she gives up her Salvationist dress and dons a conventional gown that "the ideal ... finally perished in the spotted muslin" (192). Lindsay's romance becomes like mere realist fiction, an "unlimited expanse of commonplace."

Duncan's novels defend ideal values against the commonplace, the merely real, in both technique and thematic content. They create a narrator who challenges the conventional portrayal of ideality, while still asserting its importance, in concert with the idealist philosophers who defined the tenor of Canadian intellectual life in Duncan's day. Her novels self-consciously write against the growing materialism that she associated with the US and Britain. The introduction of the colonial point of view on reality challenges the "drift of modern consciousness" with a view from the margin.

CHAPTER FOUR

Literary Feminism:
The Woman Question
and the Modern Heroine

Sara Jeannette Duncan would not have called herself a feminist. While the term was current during her lifetime, designating "a perspective which recognizes the right of women not only to an increased public role, but also to define themselves autonomously,"[1] for Duncan and her contemporaries in Canada it was reserved for those who exhibited "quite an extreme degree of commitment to women's issues."[2] Duncan was not an active crusader for women's rights; if asked about her life's work, she would probably have called herself simply a literary artist. But the artist was a woman, and that made a difference to the art.

The difference is implicit in her approach to aesthetic and imperial questions. Duncan challenges conventional formulations of women's lives in narrative; she rewrites the romance script that confines female characters to passive roles and to the happy ending of marriage. She rewrites the present and the future of the Empire, empowering the colonized, preferring feminine sentiment over abstract diplomacy, and giving women a special role to play in international politics. Duncan's support for the aims of the "woman movement" is overt in her attempt to describe and redefine women's role in the public and private spheres. In her journalism, she argues for the importance of opening up opportunities for women in education, professions, and the arts. She insists that women's intellectual achievements should be judged and rewarded according to the same standards as those of men. She calls for the ballot on the basis of women's political maturity and equal rights of citizenship. In her novels she realistically depicts the life of both the ordinary woman and the career woman – the limitations, compensations, and joys of living as a single woman or a wife in a patriarchal society – creating what Ellen Moers has called "a heroic structure for the female voice in literature": literary feminism.[3]

Duncan began writing columns for women readers in the late 1880s, just as women's suffrage and access to professional education were becoming issues in major Canadian centres such as Toronto. Her experience of "the woman question" – reported in "Woman's World" and "Other People and I" in *The Globe*, "Bric-a-Brac" in the *Montreal Star*, and "Saunterings" in *The Week* – included attendance at suffrage conventions in Washington and Toronto, visits to charitable institutions run by women, and research on opportunities for women in business and professional life. At the time, feminist movements in Canada were plagued by ideological contradiction. Women stressed their equality and similarity to men, arguing that independence and self-expression are natural rights (along the line of John Stuart Mill's radical arguments in "The Subjection of Women"), but they also stressed women's moral superiority over men and their peculiar fitness, through their "natural" role, for certain roles in public life (the position set out by John Ruskin in "Of Queen's Gardens"). The argument for reforms such as female suffrage and equality before the law, based on the natural rights of women to participate in democratic society, were intermingled with arguments for women's participation in social programs based on their potential to transform the whole of society into a happy home through work and sacrifice. Most members of the "woman movement" saw no contradiction between the two arguments and used whichever seemed useful at any given point.[4] But the reforms that won acceptance, such as the admission of women into medical schools and the education of women teachers and social-service workers, were usually those that harmonized with the view that women's natural maternal powers should be harnessed to work for the state. The original radical assertion that women had rights equal to men's was reconciled with the traditional view of women's nature by the extension of the traditional maternal role into public life.[5]

The equal-rights argument became associated with the stereotype of the "new woman" (like the so-called radical feminist of our own time) who rejected the "natural" life of love, marriage, and children and became sour and unlovely through a life of political agitation. The historical new woman was essentially a practical person who revolted against the passivity of middle- and upper-class female life and advocated a realistic view of women's capacities for education and work.[6] She proposed reforms, including the ballot for women, that would improve women's physical and economic health and allow them to take more responsibility in their own lives and in society. Enforced idleness and repeated childbearing kept women frail and ill; the new woman advocated exercise, dress reform, and sexual abstinence. Inadequate education and social attitudes kept single women poor; the new woman proposed that financial independence should be an option for those who chose it and realistically discussed the actual conditions of single mothers, spinsters, and widows. But the stereotype of the masculine woman – the "half-woman" described by August Strindberg in his introduction to *Miss Julie*, and portrayed by Charles Dickens in Mrs Jellyby – led most suffragists and women writers to keep the new woman at arm's length.

In her journalism, Duncan agrees with the new woman that women should have the vote because they are thinking individuals who bear both the rights and responsibilities of citizenship. Duncan was one of the earliest women journalists to write in favour of the vote for women in Canada (which was not won until 1918); more conservative writers, such as *The Mail*'s Kit Coleman, did not declare for women's suffrage until over twenty years later. Duncan also agrees with the new woman on the necessity of self-development for the thinking woman, and she advocates professional training for those who desire it. She opposes feminine emotionalism and insists on standards of clear thinking within women's reform groups. Unlike the stereotypical new woman, however, she also assumes that most women are "formed for" marriage and will choose the maternal role as the most attractive and natural path of life. She reconciles the two in her insistence that women act as individuals and that the opportunities for women's action be as varied as the individual women who wish to take advantage of them.

Insofar as biographical analogy is a valid critical approach, Duncan herself can be considered an example of the new woman she depicts in her novels. She was aware of the difficulties that women faced in defining both a public and a personal role. She had faced and partially defeated sexism in her professional life, becoming the first woman hired by *The Globe* to work in its Toronto office;

she later covered Parliament as one of only two women in the parliamentary press corps. If, as most critics suggest, she depicts her own life in Advena Murchison,[7] then she had some difficulty as a young woman escaping the conventional career of marriage to a local man in her home town of Brantford. A determined author who continued to write throughout her married life, Duncan began her career as a novelist by travelling around the world without a chaperon, reporting on her adventures in Canadian newspapers and in her first book *A Social Departure*. She smoked cigarettes, rode horseback (eschewing the ladylike sidesaddle for the safer and more practical western saddle), and dressed with "a general carelessness" that "betrays the Bohemian temperament."[8] She remained childless. She handled her own business affairs and, even after her marriage, often travelled alone to Europe and North America.

In her columns for the *Montreal Star*, *The Globe*, and *The Week*, Duncan focuses on one main point concerning women: women must function as responsible adults, working to their capacities, making their own decisions, and participating fully and responsibly in the life of the community. It is significant that she uses the language of the imperialist movement, advocating the equivalent of local autonomy within the structure of a final, morally idealized authority. Both kinds of colonized groups – women within patriarchal society and colonies in the old, authoritarian Empire – must be allowed to grow up. Duncan explores such topics as working conditions for women, the lives of women professionals, and the suffrage movement, as well as fashions of dress and philosophies of interior decoration, always modifying the stereotype of women as beings with limited, mainly decorative capacities and challenging her readers to look beyond it. When a reader writes to ask for a recipe for removing freckles, Duncan replies that she has twenty-three freckles and sees no reason to remove them; she declares herself strongly against ugliness in dress or decoration and strongly for higher education. Kinds of employment and the usefulness of remunerative or charitable work to self-development and personal independence are recurring subjects in Duncan's journalism.

In an interview with Dr Alice McGillivray of the Kingston Women's Medical College,[9] Duncan focuses on the rewards of the medical profession for women. Through medical training, women discover the qualities of logic, resolution, and purpose that allow them to live up to their potential as human beings. She contrasts the purposeful lives of women graduates with the feminine stereotype supposed to be preferred by men: "Logic and resolution and purpose are not distinctly feminine qualities you are thinking, Monsieur? ... logic enough to remedy our former delightful but dismaying unreasonableness, resolution enough to prop up the feebleness of will which has always distinguished us so charmingly, and purpose enough to give aim and direction to lives that were once so actively and usefully spent in crocheting bead purses for charity fairs, would not be such a bad addition to our mental and moral capital after all."[10] Duncan recommends "this branch of usefulness" to her readers as a career for women and numbers financial independence as not the least of its rewards. In addition to the pleasures of self-respect, Dr McGillivray finds her profession a source of "unbounded opportunities for doing good among her sex."[11] Women have the edge over their male colleagues in the treatment of women, Duncan relates, because women hesitate to consult a male doctor for some complaints which they have no difficulty discussing with another woman. She reports that "treatment of male medical patients by graduates of the Women's Medical College is strongly discountenanced" by the faculty, and says that this ghettoizing of women in gynaecology and paediatrics works as a strategy for gaining acceptance for women doctors among their male colleagues as well as an opportunity for women to help themselves.

If women are to succeed in male-dominated professions, Duncan states, they must submit themselves to the logical outcome of their independence; they must no longer appeal to physical frailty, false modesty, and emotionalism as shields against the aggressive competition that characterizes life outside the home. Women doctors compete in the male world by finding a section of the market that is not being served by existing doctors; such principles must operate in business as well: "The sooner every woman who brings her labour or her merchandise to the world's great market, learns that there she may expect to find no privileges, no reservation of any field ... no consideration of any kind on account of her womanhood, the better for her and all that she does."[12] Duncan explains that women refuse to do some kinds of work, and so an oversupply of "woman-labour" and a correspondingly low wage rate exist in the few professions women deign to consider. The laws of supply and demand operate in the real world,[13] she asserts, and women must approach life realistically: "It behooves us, therefore … to think less of bewailing our injuries and more of repairing them."[14]

Modest scruples more suitable to the drawing room than the office, Duncan argues, are also an impediment to women's earning capacities. In one column, she undertakes to survey working women on their conditions of work and finds that no one will answer her questions.[15] A determination to compete with men in chosen specific professions, and a straightforward acknowledgment of the facts, Duncan argues, would improve women's ability to earn. Women must realize that, when they enter the competitive world of money-making, they have "no right to expect to be regarded as wrapped in a sentimental halo of sex."[16] The use of nicknames and diminutives by professionals is another aspect of women's work that Duncan feels introduces an inappropriate element of frivolousness. She discusses an editor of an American magazine who goes by "Mamie," a name that she feels does not indicate a professional person. "This clinging to petty dignities and endearing diminutives goes far toward putting an element of incongruity between them and their work, and gives it a character often undeservedly flippant and frivolous," she writes.[17]

Feminine weakness and modesty, emotionalism, and inability to grapple with facts are not assets to women, Duncan insists, and should not have a place in women's work or women's organizations. She criticizes the gushing emotionalism she witnesses at women's suffrage meetings: "When you sit in your place and wait for strong statement or trenchant ideas or promising plans, and Mrs A opens the deliberations by asserting with tears in her eyes that she is convinced that this is a good work and ordered of the Lord, you feels she has not speeded it towards its consummation." Such traditional feminine traits as intuition and piety should not be eradicated, she argues in the same column, but should be weighed at their true value in the real world and used critically to forward the movement for women's suffrage: "Political reform is not a matter of the simple assertion of the desire to improve, howsoever baptised with tears and sighs that resolution may be. It is a long-drawn battle where every resource of cool-headed intelligence is required … In the political field as everywhere, women will need all their moral superiority; but to ardour they must add acumen, to sincerity sagacity, and to disgust with the present conditions the ability to improve them."[18] Plans, statistics, and analysis are the stuff of reform, not simply ardour. Duncan assumes moral superiority to be an agreed defining attribute of women, but she insists that women, like all people, must not simply accept the defects of their characters nor assert those defects as strengths. Women, like men, must take responsibility for their actions and strive to eradicate those elements in themselves, as well as in society, that keep them from their full responsible life.

Duncan insists that women's suffrage is just another step along that path of development for women, not a radical reversal or a sudden change. The ballot will be a tool to help women develop firmness of purpose and intelligent critical awareness. Duncan deplores women's general lack of strong opinions and advocates the vote as a method to instill a sense of the responsibility of belonging to a community: "Why is it that we have so little faith in our own opinions, so little definiteness, accuracy, grasp? So long as acquiesence only is required of us ... why should we acquire facts and compare them? ... If our opinions are worth practically nothing, why should we form them? What we need for the strengthening of our judgement, the broadening of our interest in all matters outside the realm of sensation and sentiment is responsibility – the responsibility of the ballot."[19] Duncan specifically repudiates the idea that the vote will "free" women – indeed, everywhere she opposes the idea that freedom itself is the object of the many reforms advocated under the blanket phrase "emancipation of women." Instead of freedom to behave as they will, Duncan says, women want the responsibility to behave like independent, mature citizens. Work for women symbolizes not freedom from marriage or from responsibility but the less tangible benefits of growth beyond "the affectionate tyranny that supported us in indolence" and away from "the foolish falsity of the ideas that made such a life the most honourable among women." Like work outside the home, the ballot will increase women's effort and responsibilities, but in a way that is consistent with their status as mature and independent beings: "And now we ask for the franchise, not by way of emancipation, as its intelligent exercise would certainly add another burden to the rest that have been laid upon us by our own solicitation ... Women's request for the ballot, however, as far as one can ascertain, is not based upon any hope of emancipation thereby ... but is a simple declaration that the sex has reached that point of intelligence that will permit the useful exercise of a public spirit, and is desirous of accepting the duties and responsibilities that grow out of it."[20] In rejecting the term "emancipation," Duncan also rejects the stereotype of the suffragette, that ugly, masculine, aggressive advocate of dress reform and violent social revolution. Duncan specifically counters that stereotype in her coverage of the National Suffrage Convention held in Washington in 1886. Her article focuses on the individuality of the women delegates in attendance and their powers of mature intellectual consideration.[21]

The pages of the *Indian Daily News* were often a forum for commentary on issues related to the status of women during the time that Duncan and her husband, Everard Cotes, gave the paper its editorial direction. The paper printed a series of articles by Clementina Black, "Women under Victoria," which surveyed the progress of women in gaining political, legal, educational, and marital rights. Editorials argued in favour of granting degrees to women, even from those most conservative institutions Oxford and Cambridge; the paper also followed the progress of various women's-suffrage bills in Parliament and reported on the demonstrations of the suffragists.[22]

SUCH BALD STATEMENTS of the feminist viewpoint undergo a necessary transformation when included in an artistically successful modern novel. Feminist polemics provided a standpoint from which Duncan regarded the traditions of fiction, and the artistic innovations that resulted are themselves political statement. The women in Duncan's novels are not consciously feminist, and the novels contain few of the crusading social reform passages that characterize the works of marriage reformers such as Grant Allen (*The Woman Who Did*). Rather, the feminist impulse that is evident in Duncan's early journalism is transformed into an artistic problem: how to confront the reality of women's lives in an artistic form whose traditions have been moulded by men to whom that reality was, to a large extent, unavailable. One of the defining aspects of women's writing is the portrayal of a new kind of heroine, substituting an active, thinking subject for the passive, instinctual object of romance fiction. Literary feminism, as Ellen Moers defines it and Duncan carries it out, is an attempt to construct new patterns for women's action in novels.[23]

Duncan began to represent women as characters in fictional narratives while still primarily a journalist. Her short essays describing "Mrs Brown's Callers" and "The Summer Girl" and recounting conversations between "Tiglath Pileser" and his female friends create fictional representative women of her own generation and their responses to the "new modern perplexities"[24] of women's role. The realistic representation of women in literature was something that she saw as characteristic of the modern age; in a column published on 28 October 1886 in *The Week*, she wrote that "the woman of today is no longer an exceptional being surrounded by exceptional circumstances. She bears a translatable relation to the world; and the novelists who translate it correctly have ceased to mark it by unduly exalting one woman by virtue of her sex to a position of interest in their books which dwarfs all the other characters ... The novel of today is a reflection of our present social state. The women who enter into its composition are but intelligent agents in this reflection, and show themselves as they are, not as a false ideal would have them" (772). She calls for a new kind of heroine who is no longer "the painted pivot of a merry-go-round" but who, like herself, is an independent, thinking woman who is aware of the social conventions that limit her actions and is conscious of challenging those conventions. Her first novel, based on newspaper accounts of her trip around the world with fellow journalist Lily Lewis, creates a character who consciously challenges the conventions of everyday life as a woman, a "travelling heroine"[25] whose experience of taking care of herself and of learning things unknown to her elders gives her a basis of personal power upon which to overturn the traditional view of young ladies.

S.J.D., the narrator of *A Social Departure*, declares that she has no great goal when she begins her trip around the world; but because "it was unheard of that two young women should go wandering aimlessly off to the other side of the globe" (10), the project of writing newspaper articles and later a book based on her trip is proposed as a ruse to gain family support for the project. She says that "we went chiefly to be amused" (92) in ways not available to young ladies confined within the conventional expectations of Anglo-Saxon families. However, the more serious purpose of the trip is indicated by the dedication to Mrs Grundy, patron saint of the "conventionalities" and symbol of the view that young ladies must be "protected" by men. S.J.D. and Orthodocia plan to prove that young ladies can travel quite well alone, thank you very much, without endangering their persons or their reputations. The success of their venture is confirmed on the last page, when Orthodocia's mother asks S.J.D. whether she thinks, "as a result of all [her] experiences, that it is entirely safe and wise for young ladies to travel by themselves?" The narrator concludes that "it must always depend upon the young ladies themselves." The most lasting effect of the excursion is Orthodocia's engagement to her cousin, which, as Orthodocia points out, "might have happened anywhere" (417).

Both young women manage to be thoroughly amused without leaving Canada; they ride on the cow catcher of a CPR train down the far side of the Rockies and walk up to a glacier in the company of a schoolboy who sets limits upon their adventurous designs as being improper for ladies. Orthodocia, although her name indicates otherwise, is hardly a captive of convention; Duncan introduces her exploring the beach in Yucatan, exasperating her chaperon by gambolling in the wet sand searching for conch shells with little regard for the appearance of "her front breadth" or her rear one. Although treated by the narrator as flighty and inexperienced, Orthodocia invests in a town lot in Vancouver during their two-week stay and realizes a profit of forty pounds by buying from one agent to sell to another.

The novel was written "primarily and particularly for the sex that loves to shop" (137), as the narrator reveals in her discussion of shopping in Japan; one presumes that the contents of the book were thus dictated by Duncan's sense of what her primarily female audience would enjoy. Details of housekeeping, styles of dress, manners, and general impressions of landscape dominate, but significant comments on the position of women are also included. With the Western idea of dress reform uppermost in her mind, the narrator comments on the recent adoption of Western dress by Japanese women: "Orthodocia declared that the size of their waists was entirely incompatible with dining on the floor without the most appalling tortures, and she spoke with conviction. We learned, though, that they have not yet fully entered the bonds of servitude, that the comfortable *kimono* is still in a convenient cupboard for private wear, and the gorgeously-embroidered *obis* are not yet all sold to the curio dealers. They are still experimenting, still amused; and nobody seems to have told them that they are trying to do what we have concluded to try to undo" (125). Duncan favours the oriental kimono, for those who are committed to oriental manners, as the most practical and most comfortable attire for sitting on the floor or bowing in greeting.

The greatest change in the status of the two travellers occurs when Orthodocia's cousin Jack Love turns up in India with the transparent intention of proposing marriage to Orthodocia. His precipitous arrival was prompted, Orthodocia believes, by his dislike of her travelling without a man; she is insulted by his "impertinence": "So I told him – very politely and blandly, and *quite* ignoring his argument – what a delightful trip we'd had so far, and how kind everbody'd been; and ... what a relief it was not to have a man bothering about the luggage labels, and feeling injured because he's kept waiting" (345). When Jack Love finally reaches past Orthodocia's prickly independence to propose, another difficulty arises: if Orthodocia marries before the trip concludes, her travelling companion will be unfairly saddled with a chaperon (the ceremony unfailingly having the effect of imposing conventionality upon its participants). Happily, the wedding is postponed until the two reach England, and their object of completing the trip without supervision is preserved.

The travelling heroines of *A Social Departure* learn that definitions of appropriately feminine dress and behaviour vary from country to country; in the "international" novels that follow *A Social Departure*, these cultural differences are pursued. Mamie Wick of Chicago knows that "in England, an unmarried person of my age is not expected to talk much, especially about herself" (AG, 1). Mamie tries to fit in with British customs by seeming to speak only of neutral, safe topics and disguising her judgment that England itself is "the Zoo" she observes. Her novel departs from "approved models of discussion for young ladies" (AG, 2) in Britain, but she excuses her foray into male preserves on the grounds that she wants her book to be interesting! She greets specimens of the British young lady in the home of her "relation" Mrs Portheris; their long, straight hair and buttoned dresses reveal them to be the victims of a vigorous course of "bringing up," English style. Similarly, Mary Trent of *Cousin Cinderella* remarks on the athleticism, reticence, and remarkably pink-and-white complexions of British girls, which make them seem much younger than their North American contemporaries.

The stereotype of the heroine as young, beautiful, and competent forms the background for reading another "travelling heroine," Miss Lavinia Moffat of *Vernon's Aunt*. Miss Moffat is an unmarried woman who undertakes an unaccompanied trip to India with expectations of exotic adventures. From this description she might be one of the heroines of Duncan's earlier best-seller *A Social Departure*. However, Miss Moffat illustrates the reality that not all women are twenty and beautiful: she is forty-two, a spinster, and rather sure of her ability to guide the rest of the world on questions of courtesy to middle-aged ladies. Just as Miss Moffat is not the sort of heroine the reader expects, India is not quite what Miss Moffat expects; her civil-servant nephew seems in no physical danger and her ride on an elephant is uneventful. The romance that is required by the conventions of the popular novel does materialize in a roundabout way in the person of Mr Ali Karam Bux, whose attempts to gain Miss Moffat's assistance in a legal matter are misinterpreted as a proposal of marriage. Even the animal that Miss Moffat hears chewing in the dark of her tent in Nudiwallah turns out to be no more exotic than a stray cat with a mutton bone from the kitchen tent.

As in the other novels, the reader is made aware of the challenge to her social and literary expectations by the self-consciousness of the narrative voice. Miss Moffat is writing her adventures for our benefit, and she often comments on literary conventions in order to caution the reader against them. Travelling across Europe by train, she describes her experience of officers at the Italian stations: "There were officers, too, at the various stations, just such Italian officers in cocked hats, and swords, and long cloaks as one reads of in novels, but, also judging from the novels, I expected more from them in the way of impertinent advances than I saw. In works of fiction lady travellers through Italy are always subjected to stares and smiles ... but that I now believe a literary artifice" (11). Miss Moffat's suspicion of literary conventions that claim to represent reality is transferred to the reader, who begins to suspect that most literary depictions of women leave something to be desired.

Miss Moffat's story does not end with a marriage; in fact, it has no conventional form of happy ending at all. Like many of Duncan's novels, *Vernon's Aunt* challenges the possibilities for the resolution of narrative from the colonial point of view. In her essay "Outworn Literary Methods," Duncan uses Thomas Carlyle's

clothes metaphor to portray traditional narrative patterns as "cast-
off garments" that still live in "the attic of every writer's brain,
cobwebbed and dusty from their long retirement from public usefulness"; "very well he knows they are there, but he is much too
tender a parent to send his offspring forth into a gibing world
tricked out in them." In an attempt to express the "practical spirit
of the age" and to make method conform to matter, the modern
novelist must discard "the old rules by which any habitual reader
of fiction would prophesy truly at the end of the third chapter how
the story would 'come out.'"[26] No one could predict how *Vernon's
Aunt* would "come out"; the old kind of heroine, as well as the old
kind of narrative, are discarded in order to make a new kind of
story.

The happy ending of the sentimental romance had been an issue
for the American realist movement, and William Dean Howells and
Henry James both deplored the necessity of tying up all the threads
for the reader in the last few pages of the novel. Dramatic method
seemed to demand that the novel appear as a window on the eternal
flow of life, rather than as an artificial construct that somehow
ended happily at the finish of the requisite number of pages. Duncan uses the controversy to challenge literary convention from the
colonial feminine point of view at the end of *An American Girl in
London* and *Those Delightful Americans*. In *American Girl*, Mamie
Wick remains unaware that Charlie Mafferton looks upon her as
a future bride until the last chapter; when she finally realizes his
intentions, she hurriedly boards the first ship home, explaining
that she is already engaged. After spending three hundred pages
establishing the expectation of a happy ending, the novel deflates
that expectation in one short chapter. In *Those Delightful Americans*,
the happy ending is totally different from what the reader has been
led to expect. The four young American travelling companions of
Carrie Kemball, an Englishwoman, finally make up two completely
"unsuitable" couples, and the narrator is as surprised as the reader.
Lorne Murchison's unresolved fate at the end of *The Imperialist* may
also be an experiment in challenging traditional narrative form by
leaving the ending of the novel open.

The happy ending of *The Simple Adventures of a Memsahib* occurs
at the beginning of the novel, when Helen Peachey meets, falls in
love with, and becomes engaged to "young Browne" all in the the
first chapter. As becomes a heroine in a new kind of story, Helen

also encounters a complex of new ideas about feminine behaviour as she tries to adapt to Anglo-Indian society in Calcutta. She must learn not to treat her rudimentary knowledge of Hindi as an accomplishment suitable to her sex and class; she must subdue her desire for a picturesque home and garden until after her husband's cautious inspection of drains and compounds. She no longer runs her own household, keeps accounts, or even disciplines her servants; all of the pursuits that characterize an ordinary woman in England are either impossible or unfashionable. Helen eventually adapts to the new Anglo-Indian convention of femininity, attends Sunday tennis parties, and entertains young men; she becomes a "memsahib like another": "She has lost her pretty colour, that always goes first, and has gained a shadowy ring under each eye ... To make up, she dresses her hair more elaborately, and crowns it with a little bonnet which is somewhat extravagantly 'chic'" (308). However, the change is not wholly frivolous – the memsahib has also to face the possibility of disease and death, prolonged separation from her husband, and the sense of being an alien in her place of residence: "There is a shade of assertion about her chin that was not there in England, and her eyes – ah, the pity of this! – have looked too straight into life to lower themselves as readily as they did before" (308).

THE MEMSAHIB is a heroine of a unique type in most Anglo-Indian fiction: a woman starved for company, identified with her husband's career, yet resourceful in emergencies, showing a physical and emotional strength developed by necessity and a peculiar disregard for the proprieties. Duncan was particularly aware of the stereotype of the memsahib drawn by Rudyard Kipling,[27] an inconstant flirt who compensates for her homesickness by carrying on tender friendships with young subalterns. She satirizes it in Set in Authority in the character of Mrs Arthur Poynder Biscuit who, contemplating her future life in India, had looked forward "to the many interesting situations from which she should extricate herself within a hair's breadth of compromise; but always with the hair quite visible" (36); the reality she encounters in an isolated hill station, peopled with burly military officers and harried administrators, is disappointingly tame. The contrast to Mrs Biscuit is the "chota-mem," the little memsahib whose appearance suggests the appreciation of life that hardship has brought her: "She was a thin little, white little thing, who made no pretence of doing her hair, but put a natural flower in it, and wore for further ornament a necklace of amber beads and a very constant smile – the kind of little thing one was instinctively sorry for until one saw in her eyes that she not only had any amount of pluck, but that she enjoyed life as well as anybody – the 'chota-mem,' the keen little chota-mem of Anglo-India!" (35). Mrs Perth MacIntyre, the narrator of *The Simple Adventures of a Memsahib*, who has had to sacrifice new gowns for her children's education and who sees her husband's friends and partners dying of tetanus and cholera, is the kind of heroine that Duncan makes of her English wives in India.

The narrator of "A Mother In India" is the most remarkable of Duncan's memsahib-heroines and, in some ways, one of her most remarkable women. She is a partner in a marriage that demands all of her resources of love and ingenuity and is completely satisfying emotionally. Her early life in India is characterised by near-poverty, social ostracism, illness, fear, and disappointment; it is alleviated only by the support and love of her husband: "To find out a husband's virtues," she says, "you must marry a poor man".[28] When her new baby is ordered to England, the narrator is offered the choice of the role of wife or of mother;[29] she chooses, without hesitation, to give up her "natural" role of mother to remain a wife. In consequence, she loses the opportunity to be a mother to her child, or indeed to be a mother at all.

Duncan describes the emotional conflict of the memsahib's two roles of wife and mother. She experiences the guilt of having given up her child; on her first visit to England, she resolves to resume her natural role and fantasizes about forcibly abducting Cecily from her home with her father's spinster aunts: "My days and nights as the ship crept on were full of a long ache to possess her; the defrauded tenderness of the last four years rose up in me and sometimes caught at my throat" (5). She finds identity in her role as mother: "I dried my tears and expanded, proud and pacified. I was her mother!" (5). However, the child rejects her unfamiliar overtures, running back to her aunts: "The most natural thing in the world, no doubt" (5) the disappointed mother remarks dryly.

Jessica Arden and Ruth Pearce of *Set In Authority* are two different sorts of memsahibs, both trying to carve out a kind of vocation for themselves in a society that denies to women any function but the social and familial. But neither of the two different roles – conventional wife and unconventional career woman (or "pundita," as Sir Ahmet Hossein says) – brings the happiness of an integrated personal and professional life.

Jessica Arden, wife of the Chief Commissioner of Ghoom in Bengal, is the perfect official's wife, trying to "'make it pleasant' in Pilaghur, as the wife of a Chief Commissioner is expected to make it pleasant" (28). Her talents for arranging his home, caring for his children, and creating pleasant relations among the few Europeans in Pilaghur are ignored by her husband, who deprecates her social skills and laments the lack of a wife who could participate in his intellectual endeavours. Her pathetic attempts to keep up with his reading and his interests highlight the lack of appreciation for traditional "woman's work" in the home; Arden does not recognize her worth until after her death.

Dr Ruth Pearce, Arden's independent woman friend, is the opposite of Jessica Arden. As a single woman and a professional, she has no settled place in Pilaghur society: "The table of precedence does not provide for demi-official lady doctors, having been invented before they were" (34). She makes her own place by becoming friends with the commissioner, a relationship that the European community regards as morganatic. She participates in Arden's friendship with Sir Ahmet Hossein and manages in a friendly way to inspire philosophical discussions, which she offers to her friend like gifts. Yet she can relate to Arden only on the ground of their shared ideals; when he admits that he feels sexual desire, she ends their friendship. While Jessica Arden's efforts to "make it pleasant" in the conventional wifely way draw her away from her husband, Ruth Pearce's vocation and spirituality also keep her from a satisfying union with the man she loves.

Like the memsahibs who follow their husbands to India, many of Duncan's heroines express their heroic impulses through their particular kind of love for a man. Advena Murchison of *The Imperialist* and Hilda Howe and Alicia Livingstone of *The Path of a Star* express their individuality by pondering the role of wife, choosing a man who is worthy of their respect and love, and trying to win him. The heroines are confused; they vacillate between expressing their desire openly and playing the role of the sentimental, self-sacrificing heroine who gives up her desire. In both novels, the outcome is also ambivalent; while self-expression is rewarded with marriage, so is passivity.

The Imperialist illustrates the link between the social conventions that restrict women's actions and the literary conventions that prescribe the proper deportment of a romantic heroine. Duncan evokes the stereotype of the passive, decorative heroine in Dora Milburn, who is blond, perfectly dressed, "reticent," and endowed with all the requisite accomplishments such as piano playing and flirting. However, Dora jilts the hero, Lorne Murchison, in favour of his superficial British friend Alfred Hesketh, and Duncan creates a new heroine in Lorne's sister Advena, who is active, independent, and intellectual. Catharine Sheldrick Ross sees Advena's later lapse into self-sacrifice as a flaw in Duncan's execution,[30] but Advena's attempt to conform to romance stereotype by sacrificing her love for Hugh illustrates her allegiance to the old ideals and her inability to see how to embody them in the new world. Advena, in writing her own life script, casts herself in the stereotyped role of sacrificial heroine, seeing herself a martyr to Hugh's honour and declaring that, through becoming a "friendship of spirit," their love will be purified of the body. Advena, however, does not finally submit to the stereotype, realizing that the pose of the self-sacrificing heroine is satisfying only in novels; she eventually goes to Hugh with her discovery of "what is possible and what is not" (250). Literally brought back to her senses after a meeting with Christie Cameron, she expresses "the desire of her heart" in no uncertain terms: "Send her away!" (250). Advena becomes a new kind of heroine, one who recognizes her own desire and her human need; she rejects the passivity of the heroine and actively pursues the "desire of her heart." It is significant, however, that Advena's pursuit of Hugh does not win him; only the sanction of the community, in the form of Dr Drummond's intervention, can finally unite the two lovers.

The new reality of women's lives also clashes with the stereotype of the passive heroine in *The Path of a Star*. Like *The Imperialist*, *The Path of a Star* has two heroines: Alicia Livingstone and Hilda Howe, the former a member of conventional Calcutta society and the latter a talented actress. Both women consciously choose the men they plan to marry, but they adopt very different strategies to win them. Hilda openly expresses her desire for the celibate clergyman Stephen Arnold; Alicia Livingstone, who falls in love with the socialite

Duff Lindsay, takes the more traditional course of self-sacrifice by refusing to declare her feelings and actually helping Lindsay to marry someone else. Hilda scolds her: "We are an intolerably self-sacrificing sex ... They've taught us well, the men; it's a blood disease now, running everywhere in the female line ... It's a deformity, like the dachshund's legs" (99). Alicia proposes to sacrifice her love for the happiness of Lindsay's life, and Hilda will have none of it. "And what about the happiness of yours? Do you imagine it's laudable, admirable, this attitude? Do you see yourself in it with pleasure?" (99). Hilda insists that Alicia use her own powers of judgment to condemn Lindsay's proposed marriage and thwart it.

Both women win the love of their chosen men. Although Arnold dies before his love for Hilda is consummated, his final words as she attends his death bed several months later indicate that she has won her point: "I would have married you" (308), he says. When he dies, he repudiates his celibacy: "He trusted to the new wings of his mortal love to bear his soul to its immortality" (309). Alicia also wins her lover, Lindsay, who finally recognizes her loyal support as repressed love.

Hilda is the focus of the novel, which seems to imply a value judgment in favour of her forthright behaviour and her choice to pursue her vocation – yet that judgment is undercut by Alicia's success. The story embodies the contradictions of Duncan's feminism by creating a new, independent heroine but tacitly approving the traditional, self-sacrificing role as well.

Duncan creates another kind of heroine in the female artist. She depicts writers in Elfrida Bell and Janet Cardiff of *A Daughter of Today* and an actress in Hilda Howe of *The Path of a Star*. In these novels the female artist must work to overcome the emotionalism, pettiness, smallness, and self-effacement of the traditional feminine personality to create art that is essentially androgynous. The necessity of the artist overcoming the limitations of her feminine gender is explored in *A Daughter of Today*, as Elfrida Bell tries to learn to paint at Lucien's art studio in Paris. Lucien praises the sketches of Elfrida's rival Nadie by saying, "In you, mademoiselle ... I find the woman and the artist divorced. That is a vast advantage – an immense source of power" (21). He criticizes Elfrida's work because she cannot separate it from her selfconscious awareness of her sex:

"Your drawing is still lady-like, your colour is still pretty, and *sapristi!* you have worked with me a year!" (23).

Elfrida is so sure of the dominance of an independent, sexless genius in her that she scorns what her friend Janet calls love, especially its physical basis. She declares that marriage is probably a necessity "from the point of view of the species," but that "for women it is degrading – horrible!" (157). For her, "the only dignity attaching to love as between a man and a woman [is] that of an artistic idea," a view that she holds with such literalness that she alienates Janet Cardiff, who hopes to die a grandmother (154). The idea that the physical act may be part of a spiritual experience she dismisses as the romanticization of a biological urge that mankind shares "with the mollusks" (158). Elfrida believes that Janet's idea of love is "pure self-flattery" (158).

The androgyny of artistic genius is made even more clear in *The Path of a Star*, a novel that creates two kinds of geniuses in the actress Hilda Howe and the Clarke brother Stephen Arnold. Both characters are repeatedly described as having attributes usually associated with the opposite sex: Hilda Howe laughs "like a man" (46); Stephen Arnold "flavoured what he said, and made it pretty, like a woman" (51); his face is almost "womanish in its plainness" (25). Moreover, both of these androgynous figures manage to forget the implications of gender in their everyday lives: Stephen Arnold is a celibate Anglican priest, whose cassock seems to symbolize his genderless state, and Hilda asserts that she is quite able to respect her leading man as an artist, even though he tries to seduce her. Duff Lindsay brings her down to earth by commenting, "You have a fine disregard for the fact that artists are men when they are not women" (9). Hilda replies "with ... real dejection, 'It *is* a hideous bore'" (9).

Hilda not only thinks of other artists as beings unencumbered by gender but she also projects sexlessness herself. Lindsay, who has known her for two years and is clearly attracted to her, questions why he has not fallen in love with her. He comes to the conclusion that the reason is that he thinks of her as a companion or a friend rather than as a woman: "I think it must be because she's such a confoundedly good fellow" (21). Lindsay continues to treat Hilda as a friend, promptly falling in love with Laura Filbert, and ignores Hilda until he needs her again.

The reason that genius can, and to some extent must, be

genderless is bound up in Duncan's theory of art. Art reaches up to an ideal plane, beyond the corporealities of this world. The work of art is beyond decay, Duncan argues in a column on genius, even though it is achieved using corporeal media, and its essence belongs to the realm of the spiritual.[31] Presumably, gender itself is one of those corporealities that is mutable and does not correspond to an ideal in itself.

Yet, even though the process of artistic creation is genderless, and the work itself bears no traces of the gender of its author, the artist herself is corporeal and must operate in a fallen world. Duncan continues: "The genius stands apart, shrouded and still perhaps, save for the voice of the pen, the brush or the chisel; the man goes in and out among his fellows and they all know him."[32] Elfrida falls in love with Kendall despite her scorn of such emotions; Hilda falls in love with Arnold and finds she cannot endure that love as a merely spiritual construct. Both finally realize that they want a physical as well as a spiritual union, though only Hilda has the self-knowledge to demand it of Arnold.

The other main problem determined for women artists by their gender is the depiction of what Elfrida calls "the nudities" in works of art. Hilda Howe is condemned by Calcutta society for acting in a play called A Woman of Honour in which she appears as a principal in the depiction of extra-marital affairs. "So disgustingly real" (15) remarks a Calcutta matron who attended the play without first ascertaining whether it was suitable for her party of unmarried girls and subalterns. Hilda's art appears in The Path of a Star as a problem of balancing popular taste with ideal values; Hilda appears once on stage as a prostitute (Mary Magdalene) and again as a modern woman locked in a loveless marriage. She does not scruple about the conventional appearances of the characters she depicts; she simply tries to lift the material into an ideal reality. The price of such devotion to truth is ostracism by most respectable Calcutta citizens. Even Stephen Arnold is repulsed by the repertoire of Hilda's acting company, and he encourages her, for the sake of her own soul, to leave acting and join the sisters of the Baker Institution.

Elfrida's view of art not only includes the immoral but also thrives upon it, and she argues with Janet Cardiff over the inclusion of criminals and bêtes humaines in serious fiction. Elfrida begins to live by her own views when she joins a burlesque troupe in order to research the lives of the ladies of the chorus line. Even though the work that results is successful, Elfrida's British friends find her enjoyment of the role of high-kicker vulgar, and they judge her sympathetic questioning of her fellow women as exploitation. There is some evidence that Elfrida's experience among the desperately poor and ostracized women of the troupe begins to humanize her: she starts to understand the reality of exploitation and money; she does not romanticize the pain the women feel in the way that she romanticizes her own pain. However, Kendall, Janet, and Lawrence Cardiff lose all respect for Elfrida simply because she chooses to write on what they see as a vulgar subject, without regard for the merit of the work or its effect on Elfrida as an independent person.

Duncan's creation of the new kind of heroine who attempts to gain self-definition through travel, love, and the vocation of the artist demonstrates how her artistic vision is shaped by the feminist principles that she elucidates in her journalism. The novels evoke and then challenge both the social and the literary conventions that limit women's actions; they question stereotypes of female behaviour, be they traditional or feminist, and allow the female characters to develop individually. Duncan's depiction of women parallels her representation of political colonialism; she reveals the singular point of view available only to those who have experienced life beyond the definitions imposed by the centre, and she looks to ideals to help create the unity that will allow men and women to continue to work together and to mitigate the increasing focus on the pragmatic, material aspects of life.

CHAPTER FIVE

Democracy and Monarchy: "The Development between the Two"

Sara Jeannette Duncan's point of view, drawn from her Canadian intellectual roots and her feminism, provided the context for her engagement with the central Victorian question of democratic reform. Canadian idealism seemed to be incompatible with colonial democracy. Idealism is essentially the philosophy of monarchic (or meritocratic) government, because it assumes that certain individuals (heroes in Thomas Carlyle's terms) are able to see beyond the material world into a world of absolute truth, and that such individuals are best able to govern. But, throughout the nineteenth century, the basis of governmental power in Britain and the US increasingly became the middle- and working-class voter, who demanded immediate reforms in economic policy. Democracy seemed to dictate that all parties create policy with the short-term goal of winning votes, which was best achieved by appealing to the self-interest of the voter. To Canadian idealists, who believed that reform should proceed conservatively through transcendence of self and adherence to eternal principles, democracy seemed to be government by anarchic selfishness.

Canadians felt that a simple choice between democracy and monarchy was not their only option. Monarchy and democracy were rooted in British history; many felt, however, that the modern British government had adulterated the original ideas. Canadians thought that they could preserve both monarchy and democracy in their own form of parliamentary democracy. At the beginning of the Victorian era, Canada was essentially an agricultural colony of small landholders and had a burgeoning industrial base that prospered by serving the needs of farmers. The advent of free education and responsible government made Canadians confident about democracy, but the example of unrestrained democracy in the US made the link with the British monarchy of equal importance. Many Canadians felt that in their government they had reconciled the idealist belief in absolute principles of government with democratic practice. Canadians such as George Parkin and G.M. Grant[1] shared a hostility to republican democracy, which Grant described in *Ocean to Ocean*: "All appeals are made to that which is lowest in our nature, for such appeals are made to the greatest number and are more likely to be immediately successful. The character of public men and the national character deteriorate. Neither elevation of sentiment, nor refinement of manners, is cultivated. Still more fatal consequences, the very ark of the nation is carried periodically into heady fights; for the time being, the citizen has no country; he has only his party, and the unity of the country is constantly imperilled."[2] Grant felt that democratic methods should be integrated with monarchical principles, and in that way the country would avoid the extremes that republican democracy seemed to encourage. Similarly, in his speech presenting the confederation agreement to the parliaments of Canada East and West, John A. Macdonald pointed out that Canada has the best of both British and American systems of government by profiting from the stability of monarchy while incorporating responsible, federal government.[3] The British North America Act seemed to considerably advance the concept of federal government over the US constitution by creating a government that was both democratic and "strong, stable, and above the people."[4]

Duncan links Canada's ability to preserve ideals in the face of growing materialism with the specifically feminine duty of reconciliation between warring extremes. For Duncan, the process of bringing monarchy and democracy together also involved the reconciliation of the great monarchy, England, with her former colony, the great democracy of the United States. Canada, by showing that a reconciliation of the styles of government was possible, provided a model for making up the "family quarrel" that was the American Revolutionary War. Duncan thus sees Canada performing a specifically feminine role – bringing the two warring members of the family together – when she emphasizes Canada's linking of monarchy and democracy in government.

Allowing women greater participation in the political process opens politics to the particular virtues that Duncan felt characterized women. The strength of women's emotions and their ability to empathize as well as the moral superiority often imputed to women in the late nineteenth century, allow Rani Janaki, Mary and Pamela Pargeter, and Advena Murchison to make tangible contributions to the political theories propounded by their men. While democracy, in the form of the vote, does not yet extend to women in these books, the women are already taking part in political life on an intellectual and intuitive level.

DUNCAN was a contemporary of the so-called Confederation group of writers in Canada, and, like Charles G.D. Roberts, Archibald Lampman, Bliss Carman, and Duncan Campbell Scott, she grew to intellectual maturity exposed to debates about nationhood and the nature of colonial government. She moved to India in 1891, where she witnessed the growth of the Indian nationalist movement and the attempted reforms of Lord Curzon during his term as viceroy from 1898 to 1905. In many ways, the views of democratic reform that she expresses in her novels reflect conservative attitudes prevalent in Canada at the turn of the century: the idealization of Canada; distrust of the voter and, especially, the middle class; suspicion of educated Indians; and the perceived violent intentions of some parts of the nationalist movement. They also reveal her "tory reformist" concern for the poor and an accompanying sympathy for the national aspirations of Indians that may have grown from her Canadian experience.

Duncan wrote four major novels that treat the issue of democracy and its relation to social reform: *His Honor, and a Lady* (1896), *The Imperialist* (1904), *The Burnt Offering* (1910), and *The Consort* (1912). The novels span a period of sixteen years and show her continued interest in political issues throughout her career. Tausky and Fowler suggest that the novels show the development of increasing bitterness over the defeat of Imperial Federation and aristocratic government in Canada and England, but certain ideas remain consistent. All four novels dramatize the selfishness inherent in democracy, whether exhibited through "partyism," personal ambition, or desire for monetary gain; all show how government informed by culture and imagination, rather than simple expediency, must be the aim of political action. However, all four novels also show the defeat of ideal government by the flaws of human nature.

DUNCAN'S CRITIQUE of democratic government centred in the belief that democracy appealed to the selfishness of the voter. The phil-istine middle classes seemed to vote only for measures that would increase their profit margins; the lower classes voted for revenge against their masters and for immediate relief of their situation. Parties were merely unprincipled factions whose only aim was to attain power and to reward supporters. So-called higher values such as truth, altruism, adherence to principle, and even good manners no longer seemed to be elements of public life. In an 1887 article for *The Week*, Duncan sets out her views on democratic government. "We are ostensibly engaged in an unending struggle for ideal government," she writes, but we are hampered in that struggle by our own, fallen natures. "Since government is but the net and general expression of our balanced imperfections as indi-viduals," no extension of the franchise can be a panacea for the ills of government. Universal manhood suffrage (and colonial self-government) is a worthwhile goal but it is not a solution. "When human limitations were laid down in the beginning, the decree that made the greatest happiness of the greatest number[,] a prin-ciple forever to be obscured by the practice intended to illustrate it, was in the nature of a tight, hard bandage across our prehistoric eyes. It has never been removed, and it never will be, for it is as old and as vital as selfishness; although, of course, there is not to be found in any legislative chamber a politician who will acknowl-edge the least imperfection in his vision." While the "right and justice" of universal manhood suffrage was "apparent enough" to Duncan, "the possible wrong and injustice of it lies *perdu* in the common impression that the evils of legislation can be swept away on the tide of universal suffrage."[5] Democracy is a new stage in the struggle towards the ideal, but one that must be undertaken with caution, for it cannot be an improvement unless humanity itself can be improved.

In late-nineteenth-century Canada, party discipline seemed to be a manifestation of selfishness, and it led to a revulsion against "partyism" among idealist politicians and, to some extent, among the general populace. Party loyalty seemed to require corruption, for a party politician might be instructed to vote against personal principles. Party mechanisms for contesting elections were notoriously underhanded, and campaigning crossed the line of fair debate with personal attacks, scandal-mongering, and biased journalism. Reaction against party politics became widespread in England; Benjamin Disraeli and Herbert Henry Asquith both considered forming joint governments of "national reconciliation" or efficiency, which would do away with the wasted time and energy that party debate seemed to involve. In Canada, the Canada First movement decried the influence of party in its motto, "Country above Party."[6] Duncan's friend John Willison left his position as editor of The Globe in order to escape party influence; Goldwin Smith declares in his prospectus for The Week that the dominance of partyism in journalism spurred the creation of his magazine, to which Duncan was a major contributor.[7] G.W. Ross, an acquaintance of Duncan's who later became premier of Ontario, described the electors of Ontario as "an army of followers to whom gifts of various kinds have to be distributed; otherwise they would disband and return to their tents."[8] The "hostility to 'partyism'" was general among Canadian intellectuals[9] and persisted until the end of the century.

Duncan saw the perils of a democratic government unrestrained by monarchic ideals in US democracy. For her, the US constitution guarded what she mockingly referred to as "the sacred right of the meanest intelligence to an equal voice with the noblest in the government of a nation."[10] The corruption of American elections and the consequent sullying of politics in the public eye illustrated selfishness run rampant: "Instead of one king this enlightened nation is ruled by many bosses, who play the game of government with a single eye to their pockets, and are in no way responsible to the people, and men naturally and morally endowed to do their country good keep out of politics."[11] Furthermore, US conduct in the Spanish-American War, the Venezuelan border dispute, and in negotiations with Hawaii (all discussed in the pages of the Indian Daily News while Duncan was an editorialist there) had illustrated the axiom that Duncan quoted from Smith: "[Republican] democracy is unfitted for empire."[12]

Part of the problem of governing by democratic "selfishness" seemed to be neglect of necessary social reform. The traditional view of the aristocrat (and especially the monarch) had always contained a special awareness of the plight of the poor. The appeal of the helpless (especially women, as illustrated by Elizabeth Lount's famous appeal for the life of her husband) directly to the monarch or his representative was supposed to be the hope of the poverty-stricken workers, and was an accepted part of the British legal system. Yet the industrial revolution had eliminated the traditional relationship between master and man and had not offered a substitute; democracy, rather than restoring the responsibility of the powerful to protect the weak, had merely shifted power to the middle class and left the poor defenceless against the depredations of the capitalists. Reflecting the belief that democracy increased the vulnerability of the poor by taking away their traditional protectors, reactionary reformers such as John Ruskin,[13] Carlyle (in *Past and Present*), and even Charles Dickens (through Stephen Blackpool, the workman character in *Hard Times*) called for a return to a semi-feudal paternalistic responsibility of the rich towards the working poor.

Duncan's view of the responsibility of the rich for the poor, or the strong for the weak, partakes of the paternalism of the tory reformists and the condescension of Anglo-India. She touches on the familiar portrayal of the battered British working classes in *The Consort* and *The Imperialist*; in both she presents emigration as the best solution to British poverty. In her book of essays *On The Other Side of the Latch*, she marvels that a mere accident of fate placed her in a ruling position, with "an acute sense of undeserved superiority to coolies and postmen" (68). To be aware of her superior position, she believes, is to have two sets of nerves, "one for our own use and one at the disposal of every human failure by the wayside" (70), and she buys an unnecessary load of fuel to save both the painful difficulty of dealing with the coolie's trip back down the mountainside. For her, such paternalistic single actions that express a sense of common humanity and Christian charity are the kinds of social reform that the ordinary individual can carry out; larger, overall programs call for special leadership.

Duncan was aware that money and party support are not guarantees of responsible leadership; a leader also needs imagination. For Duncan, imagination is the ability to see beyond the material surface, to find a way to preserve important ideals and to apply them in the modern context. The concept of imagination in government was popularized by Disraeli, who presented the restoration of imagination in political life as a major part of his program of reform in the "Young England" trilogy; he felt that his books demonstrated that "imagination in the government of nations [is] a quality not less important than reason."[14] As an alternative to utilitarian liberalism, the idea of imaginative government bolstered the colonial idealist position by reasserting the importance of human intuition and compassion and denying the supremacy of material conditions in determining human history.

Duncan judges imagination to be an essential element in the Imperial Federation movement and in social reform generally. Imagination is a factor in Lorne Murchison's legal career and his political vision in *The Imperialist*: "Imagination, one gathers, is a quality dispensed with of necessity in the practice of most professions, being that of which nature is, for some reason, most niggardly. There is no such thing as passing in imagination for any department of public usefulness, even the government of Oriental races; the list of the known qualified would be exhausted, perhaps, in getting the papers set. Yet neither poet nor philosopher enjoys it in monopoly; the chemist may have it, and the inventor must; ... Lorne was indebted to it" (86). In *The Story of Sonny Sahib*, imagination is a racial characteristic of the English, for it is Sonny's "birthright to pretend, in a large, active way" (22). Lack of imagination is one of the problems of John Church in *His Honor, and a Lady*; the novelist heroine of *The Consort* uses imagination to rise above party and find a way to work for social reform outside democratic government.

Duncan explores the potential of the imaginative man for doing good within a meritocracy in *His Royal Happiness*. She creates a portrait of a future king of England who is suited to his position by nature as well as heredity. Because Alfred is open to a reconciliation with the United States, he represents both the democratic and the monarchic tendencies that have grown from the British constitution: "He was tall, and his carriage was haughty, sensitive, and his manner was shy; his features were patrician to the point of austerity. But these were appearances not readily accounted for in his character. Under them his nature was direct and humble. It would have been difficult for him to assume anything, most of all a democratic ideal, since these in a very abstract sense were already an essential part of him" (4). The prince has the manner and the appearance of a hereditary aristocrat, with the ideal virtues that

that implies, but his nature is democratic. Duncan underscores the duality of his character by giving him a uniquely significant history at Oxford: the prince democratically insists on sitting regular exams in his specialty, American history, and proves his superiority by taking a First. When he becomes king he is not content to be a figurehead; he works actively in the business of government, and manages to conclude an arbitration and mutual-defence treaty with the United States (through the agency of a Canadian friend).

Imaginative vision marked the true member of the new meritocracy; those without it were liable to do more harm than good in their attempts to lead. The professional reformer's inflexible adherence to principles (or, more often, to one principle) rather than to the general good, seemed simply destructive. Carlyle characterized single-issue reformers as believers in a "Morrison's Pill," a simple and easily applied remedy that would magically solve problems that Carlyle saw as deeply rooted in modern society. In contrast, idealists proposed a redirection of human attitudes away from the material towards the ideal. Matthew Arnold introduced the idea of two kinds of approaches to social reform, Hebraic and Hellenistic, in his essay *Culture and Anarchy*. The Hebraist is single-minded, plodding, unimaginative, and finally destructive; he operates according to rigid principles that allow no deviation. The Hellenist attempts to study the past and the ideals it displays, to obtain culture, and to reform slowly and gradually by a flexible intellectual understanding that allows no personal involvement. Roberts characterized the two kinds of reformers in an 1883 speech: "Without training the reformer is apt to be a destructionist, a physician deadly to the society he would heal. Those men are needed for the task of reform who by education, and discipline, and study of past events with their causes and their results, have acquired mental balance; who are striving to attain clear vision and calm judgement; who will know and preserve the good growth while strenuously eradicating the evil."[15] Duncan similarly divides her reformers into the Hebraic single-issue reformer and the Hellenic idealist in her novels, portraying the former as ultimately too unaware of his own limitations to be effective. In Duncan's novels, reformers such as John Church of *His Honor, and a Lady* and Anthony Andover Thame in *Set In Authority* do more harm than good; like Arnold's philistines, they have no understanding of history and so no objective measure for their own actions.

DUNCAN consistently depicts Canada as approaching an ideal of social development.[16] In 1886, she wrote that the nation had fulfilled the promise of Confederation by building a new kind of social order:

Socially Canada has no small cause to think well of herself. Her people are well educated, well read, and, on the whole, well mannered. Her aristocracy of birth is so slender, and her aristocracy of wealth so small, that, while the influence of both is unmistakably felt, neither of these invidiously operating castes obtains here to any very damaging extent. While we are largely governed by the social traditions that obtain in England, we are so far from the autocratic code of insular dictation, and so near the somewhat lax and liberal system that prevails among our cousins of the Republic, that repressive austerities are somewhat softened among us with the result of a decided gain in individuality.[17]

Duncan writes that the people of Canada are educated, self-supporting, and generally beyond the repressive misuse of aristocratic government, whether based on birth or wealth. The reason for Canada's enviable status is its ability to reconcile North American democratic freedom and equality with the British traditions inherent in monarchic government. Although governed by social traditions that have their basis in England's class system, Canadians are preserved from the abuses of hierarchy by their proximity to the US. Duncan reiterates her faith in the development of the common people of Canada in *The Imperialist*, giving an account of the "reassorting" of social classes carried out by the collegiate institute – the "melting pot" (76) of the new society – and by the Rebellion of 1837. In Duncan's fiction, the rebellion assumes a rather benign cast: the ruling aristocrats are foreclosed, succeeded in office and scattered without bloodshed (although Duncan must have been aware that this was not the case, in fact, for many of the rebels came from the Brantford area). She implies that this social shakedown is a necessary stage in the evolution of the nation: "It was a sorry tale of disintegration with a cheerful sequel of rebuilding, leading to a little unavoidable confusion as the edifice went up. Any process of blending implies confusion to begin with; we are here at the making of a nation" (47). The new society is to be one big middle class, "all hard-working folk together" (47). Although some in Elgin (notably Mrs Milburn) still insist on interpreting social relations according to the more rigid standards of a hierarchy based on "respectability" of occupation, they merely represent the distance between the ideal and the actual.

In *The Imperialist*, the results of the "process of blending" are epitomized in the farmers of Fox County: Elmore Crow, who returns from the west to help out with the family farm; Mrs Crow, who makes change at the Elgin market; the men who assemble at the Crow farm to hear Lorne Murchison's appeal for their votes. They illustrate Canada's ability to reconcile British ideals (represented in the monarch) with democratic practice. Duncan writes: "They were big, quiet, expectant fellows, with less sophistication and polemic than their American counterparts, less stolid aggressiveness than their parallels in England, if they have parallels there. They stood, indeed, for the development between the two; they came of the new country but not of the new light; they were democrats who had never thrown off the monarch" (191). Because they have not thrown off the monarch, the common people of Canada are able to respond to the vision of life beyond material values that Lorne Murchison's candidacy for the Canadian parliament symbolizes.

Although Lorne loses the election, the circumstances of his loss are uncertain. The voters do have the potential to respond to his vision of ideals beyond the commonplace; their stubborn allegiance to the Queen, which persists only as a sentimental "tether" that binds them to the royal family, still proves their ability to see beyond the merely material. Lorne lifts his audience with him during his final emotional campaign speech, even though his party workers consider the speech a failure. He appeals to their sense of ideals, and they like "being made to feel like that" (229); during a pause, the narrator tells us, "his words were vivid in their minds; the truth of them stood about him like an atmosphere" (233). Even his agent, Bingham, is overcome. In their zeal to elect their candidates, both parties tamper with the voting; who actually would have won a fair election is unclear. Lorne still finds a way to channel his energies for the good of the nation and "goes forth to his share in the task" (268) of nation building.

While English values are idealized in *The Imperialist*, England itself is not. Lorne advises Canadians to stick to England for "the moral advantage" of English history and the "human product" (98) of English evolution, but he realizes that, in political terms, England offers no model for Canada. The "hungry twelve millions" and their day-to-day existence govern the British future and scare them "out of anything but hand-to-mouth politics" (133). The mass of uneducated voters impedes the progress of imperial union (129), and the self-interested manufacturing class looks no further than its immediate profits (121). Lorne realizes that the English "patient sort of way ... and the look in their eyes, poor dumb dogs" (128) is something that he and his family were lucky to escape. Canada, not England, becomes the standard by which to judge other cultures, although it, too, is flawed.

However exemplary Canada's social organization, the nation's economic and social problems in the late nineteenth century were manifestly obvious to Duncan. Economic depression, corrupt party politics, federal-provincial squabbles, and diplomatic disputes with England and the US made chaotic commentary on the dream of nationhood; as a result, Duncan considered various alternatives proposed for Canada's trade and foreign affairs. On one of her many excursions to the US, she was a guest of Erastus Wiman, the champion of commercial union between Canada and the United States. As a columnist for *The Week*, she was probably acquainted with Smith's views on annexation as well. In 1888 she wrote, "Commercial Union, Imperial Federation, Annexation, Independence, however we would ballot for Canada's future, we cannot be deaf to the voices in the East and the voices in the West crying aloud in the hearing of ever-increasing multitudes that a change must come."[18] What that change should be, and how accomplished, however, is limited by human nature. Democracy has not solved the problems of the English-speaking world, but only changed them. Democratic individuals must learn to set their own selfish natures aside and live according to the needs of the whole of society.

IN *The Imperialist*, Canadians have undergone a peaceful transformation from colony to nation by joining the traditions of aristocratic British government to democratic self-rule. They have proved themselves part of a mature society by recognizing the ideals higher than personal gain that loyalty to the monarch represents, even if, through the structure of human nature, they fail to attain them fully. Canada becomes a standard of orderly social change that

Duncan applies to other cultures: to India in *The Burnt Offering* and *His Honor, and a Lady,* and to England in *The Consort*.

Like Canada in *The Imperialist,* India in *The Burnt Offering* is a "nascent nation" (313), but her growth to self-government is accompanied by violence. Ganendra Thakore,[19] the publisher of a revolutionary newspaper, conducts an underground school for religious terrorists aimed at freeing "Mother India" from British rule. His group finds the impetus to action in the visit of a sympathetic Labour MP, Vulcan Mills,[20] and his free-thinking daughter Joan. Increasing agitation leads to a repressive law against public assembly, which Thakore and Mills determine to test. Both are arrested, and the novel ends as Bepin Behari Dey, Thakore's disciple and Joan Mills's fiancé, tosses a homemade bomb at the viceroy and then commits suicide.

In *The Burnt Offering,* India's inability to identify a common ideal, British or Indian, is the main bar to nationhood. Thakore, although he is identified by the narrator in her depiction of his trial as the betrayed soul of India, is motivated by revenge in his agitation against British rule: his son died from disappointment after failing the civil service exam. Thakore is driven to extreme actions by intoxication "with his own direct personal influence" (78), and he seems to wield his power over the youth of India with self-absorbed glee. His disciple, Dey, is a fanatic who blindly follows Thakore to his own death. Moreover, Dey's revolutionary ardour is subject to a highly developed class sense, and he despises both Indians and English who rank below him socially. In opposition to the nationalist characters, Duncan offers Sir Kristodas and his daughter Rani Janaki, whose absorption into British culture is almost total. Both seem to lose their identities as Indians until reminded of their religious duties as Brahmins by Swami Yadava.

But the English in *The Burnt Offering* are similarly scattered and materialistic. The English as a nation have become self-indulgent and luxurious, Yadava believes, and are no longer motivated by their own ideals: "They are strangely changing, the English. An age of luxurious doubt is upon them – it has come with their great prosperity. They indulge their souls as well as their bodies. They ask questions, questions of themselves. 'Ought we?' they say. They have lost faith in their own motives" (164). Democracy in England represents part of the English loss of faith. Yadava complains that "a democratised England" is merely a "proletariat throwing India, and the soul of India, under some mean axiom made to fit its grovelling necessities of the ballot" (166). Kristodas is shocked to realize that the Indian government is under the sway of people "who had never been nearer to India than Earl's Court" (41) and who, like the Oxford free-thinkers who educated his daughter, have no belief in the future of British rule in India. Duncan makes it clear that the solution is not, however, a return to aristocratic government; Yadava and civil servant John Game both look forward to a revitalized tradition leading to self-government.

When Duncan turns to a serious social and political analysis of India's growth toward self-government in *The Burnt Offering*, she suggests a model for its development that strongly parallels Canada's growth towards self-government. Yadava continues: "When the fruit is ripe ... it drops to the ground ... they will grant us our desire, the good English, and leave to us our country. They will take some taxes, which we can very well spare, to pay an army to protect us ... the Viceroy will become a magnified Resident, very polite about the tariff, and the white rulers, as a caste, will disappear" (162–4). The new nation will be a marriage of traditions between "Mother India" and "Father England," and in the novel the first step towards self-government is acknowledgment of that fact. "We talk of the Mother as if we had but one parent ... But we are the children of England also. Can we deny it?" (165) Yadava asks. Both England and India have something of value to contribute to the new nation: "The English by their administration have given her justice, railways, political ideas. God, by my ancestors, gave her a soul. The English will leave their gifts and go, but the God of India and the soul of India ... will remain with her" (163). Although Yadava, Kristodas, and Janaki agree that British ideas are foreign to Indian culture, they also insist that "we could not do without them" (163). The attempt of the British to impose their ideals prevents social chaos; Yadava fears another French Revolution in India when the British withdraw: "First the hand against the king, then the hand against the priest – against God. As it has been in France, as it will be in Ireland" (167). Democratic self-government will come, but by goodwill and friendship between the races: "God has the emancipation of India in his hand ... but it cannot be taken away from him by force, or by fraud, or in any evil way" (162). Duncan believes that, like Canada, India is taking part in a natural growth towards self-government that will culminate in the adoption of

British institutions as native, and the establishment of a sentimental and ceremonial tie between Britain and India.

The logical outcome of the spiritual poverty of utilitarian democracy is represented in the character of Vulcan Mills. "Accustomed all his life as he was to hard chances and reserved faces" (128), Mills is overcome by the "romance" of India and the emotional adulation of Indians, and he begins to despise his working-class constituents. The "dream and the incense" increase his determination not to find any good in Britain and her traditions; in his tour of India, "he found more in a perjured policeman than in the justice of the courts ... and the corpse of a starved coolie obscured the saving of a race" (85). Michael Foley describes him as an "inverted idealist" (60) willing to tear down accepted truths in order to see utilitarianism grow, presumably along the model of the much-feared French republic. He refuses to see the signs of political violence in his Indian friends and so endangers the entire community by acting as he would in England: "At home he represents a tendency which can be taken into account with any other; but in a place like this, where things are rigid, he's bound to do harm" (15). Mills is motivated by a genuine desire for reform, but he misapplies his ideals by trying to replace British culture with the abstract principle of liberty. He is disgusted when confronted by the reality of colonial government. When a retired sepoy complains against his Indian neighbours and requests that Mills ask the king to send more Englishmen in order to keep the peace, Mills is shocked that Indians would fight among themselves, and abruptly dismisses his petitioner (171–7).

Despite his sympathy for Indian nationalism, Mills is an object of contempt for Thakore and his revolutionary group because he is so ready to criticize his own country. Thakore, who bases his revolutionary fervour on a religious tradition of India as a spiritual mother, says that Mills has "no mother, and no gods" (29). Mills quotes an English proverb – "It's an ill bird that fouls its own nest" (176) – to his Indian listeners; the significance recoils upon the speaker. Characteristically, Mills is an avid reader of *On Liberty*, but "he did not read far enough to be disappointed" (22); presumably, he ignores John Stuart Mill's disclaimer that his ideas cannot apply to India.

For Duncan, the "justice and peace, and freedom and that sort of thing" (60) that Game and his compatriots offer India are the real basis of British authority. Material improvements can go only so far; Game admits, "We are only a Government – we are not God Almighty" (92). Both the British and the Indians must learn to follow the commandments of their respective religions to "live beyond self" in order to preserve order and to better the condition of average Indians.

The community manages to grasp for ideals beyond self as a result of Dey's attempt on the viceroy's life. Relief at the viceroy's survival sweeps through a crowd waiting for his arrival, and a new sympathy is created between the government and the people in their love of the idea of monarchy. The crowd cries "God save the King" and the viceroy replies "Bande Mataram" ("Hail Motherland," the nationalist slogan taken from a poem by Bankim Chandra), showing his sympathy for the "nascent nation" (TBO, 310). In the mood of restored goodwill, the repressive laws are repealed, and a new respect for order unites the nation.

Part of the problem that Duncan dramatizes in *The Burnt Offering* is the danger of educating Indians in the ideology of democracy – British skeptical materialism. Duncan further depicts the cost of educating upper-class Indians in materialism without the leavening influence of ideals of self-sacrifice and compassion in *His Honor, and a Lady*. According to Duncan, the educated classes of India are simply the sons of the exploiters who have forced the majority of their countrymen into abject poverty, and their influence on the government of India serves merely to consolidate their own power. Consistent with her tory reformist view, she depicts the paternalistic reforms of Church, carried out in opposition to upper-class India, as the real hope of the poverty-stricken peasant.

Church, the fictional lieutenant-governor of Bengal, attempts to reduce government funding to British-style universities, using the taxes gained from the mass of peasant Indians to educate farmers in the latest agricultural techniques instead. He is defeated in what Duncan presents as an ideal aim[21] by the clamour that educated India raises in democratic England through the press and its duped parliamentary allies, and by the ambition and self-seeking of his political masters. The story prefigures Curzon's similar plan to reduce access to British-style universities in India, put forward at an educational conference in Simla in 1901.

Duncan introduces Church ironically, as a short-sighted man who sees "nothing, literally" but the road in front of him. He refuses to compromise principle, even for the laudable aim of getting his reforms implemented, and so to some extent defeats himself. A slave to duty and service, he is characterized by one of the other characters in the novel as "that objectionable ethical mixture, a compound of petty virtues. He believes this earth was created to give him an atmosphere to do his duty in; and he does it with the invincible courage of short-sightedness combined with the notion that the ultimate court of appeal for eighty million Bengalis should be his precious Methodist conscience" (49). But Church is "honest," and when, at the middle of the book, he attempts to justify his educational plan to his private secretary, he speaks sympathetically:

You and I know where the money comes from – the three lakhs and seventy-five thousand rupees – that goes every year to make B.A.s of Calcutta University. It's a commonplace to say that it is sweated in annas and pice out of the cultivators of the villages – poor devils who live and breed and rot in pest-stricken holes we can't afford to drain for them, who wear one rag the year through and die of famine when the rice harvest fails! The ryot pays, that the money-lender who screws him and the landowner who bullies him may give their sons a cheap European education. (190)

His dedication to those poverty-stricken ryots is finally the cause of his death; after a day of visiting a disease-ridden town in an attempt to raise health standards and prevent torture of prisoners by local authorities, he dies of a sudden attack of fever.

Church is also defeated by forces with democratic power: the local educated Indian, the uneducated British public, and his own party. The educated Bengali, represented by the two journalists Tarachand Mookerjee and Mohendra Lal Chuckerbutty, are to some extent examples of the literary stereotype of the "Bengali gentleman," adorned with BAs, an incomplete command of English, many superlative adjectives, and copious amounts of sweet-smelling oil. They take advantage of any opportunity to attack the government, and have little regard for traditions of true and objective journalism. They engineer a campaign for the support of the British voter, using their own inflated editorials and their connections in Britain to take the public debate to the newspapers in England.

European-style universities in India were partly supported by mission funds from English churches. Although Chuckerbutty says

"It iss [sic] not to change their religion that the Hindus go to college" (116), the pastors of religious universities preach to British constituents the spiritual necessity of the defeat of Church's plan, and the clamour they raise is enough to make the ruling party nervous. As in *The Consort*, the party impulse to retain power represents the evils of the democratic system; the letter dismissing Church from his post contains the postscript "Thus party doth make Pilates of us all" (233).

The most immediately important opposition to Church comes from his private secretary, Lewis Ancram, an ambitious and clever man whose "ideal policy toward the few score million subjects of the Queen-Empress" (104) is "one of exalted expediency" (105). Ancram resents the fact that Church ignores his advice: "He had not merely ignored the advice; he had rejected it somewhat pointedly, being a candid man and no diplomat. If he had acknowledged his mistakes ever so privately, his Chief Secretary would have taken a fine ethical pleasure in forgiving them; but the Lieutenant-Governor appeared to think that where principle was concerned the consideration of expediency was wholly superfluous" (112). Ancram's "vanity" (112) is offended; he not only withholds his true opinion of the education bill from Church, but writes a leading article for Chuckerbutty's newspaper denouncing it. The article is later quoted in England as an example of native Indian reaction, and is instrumental in Church's downfall. Ancram's betrayal is compounded by his attentions to Church's wife, a sensitive woman whom Church neglects in favour of his social program.

Although Church's program is presented favourably in the novel, Church himself is a composite of heroic virtue and very human failing. He is unable to see his wife's unhappiness or Ancram's ambitious designs. His name and his "methodist conscience" suggest an identification with the intransigent protestant reformism that influenced British policy towards suttee, female infanticide, and Indian education throughout the nineteenth century. Church is unable to see that his reforms will be overturned without popular support, and that he must cultivate "a body of public opinion, without which, as a basis, progressive enactments are not worth the paper they are written on."[22] The hero, however much a genius, must work within a fallen reality, and must take the political climate into account. In his offensively single-minded attempt to impose his reforms, Church resembles Curzon, whom Duncan criticized in an 1896 column because he did not act with the necessary expediency to get his reforms accepted; she urged him to develop the quality if his ambitions extend to the viceroyalty.[23] Her novels of Empire convey the necessity of working within local political and cultural conditions in the colonies.

However, even if Church himself is not perfect, the implications of the book remain. Social reforms to benefit the poor of India must be a first priority, and are hampered by democracy. Human society is governed by selfishness, and even those who rise above the principle of individual profit must operate in a fallen world. Western society, in its rush to worship science and give voice to the masses, has lost its direction. Church is not sure that Europeans who have supported education in India have acted correctly: "When we have helped these people to shatter all their old notions of reverence and submission and self-abnegation and piety, and given them, for such ideals as their fathers had, the scepticism and materialism of the West, I don't know that we will have accomplished much to our credit" (190). European-style education has been put "into hands that can only use it to destroy" (190), Church concludes.

The Consort depicts the necessity of going beyond selfish party loyalty in order to confront the reality of working-class life. The action in the novel takes place entirely in England, and concerns Leland Pargeter, the "consort" of the title, who runs for a seat in the Commons as a member of the State Labour Party. His candidacy is opposed by his strong and independent wife Mary, a powerful millionaire whose generosity to social causes has made her popular with the voters in her husband's constituency. The novel focuses on Pargeter's daughter Pamela, a successful novelist, who forsakes the conservative Unionist Party (and her lover, a Unionist MP) to canvass for her father. In the course of her visits to poor working-class families, she comes to realize that neither party has a monopoly on progressive policies and that the real priority of both parties should be the "lifting up of our own" (245) through a rejuvenation of British political traditions. She ends by working outside the party system as joint administrator of a philanthropic fund, creating a new place for the aristocratic impulse of *noblesse oblige* within a democratic society.

Although *The Consort* is not as specific in its explanation of political ideologies as *The Imperialist*, the politics of the novel are fairly clear. The (conservative) Unionist Party supports gradual social reform through land redistribution under the capitalist system; Mary Pargeter's scheme for agrarian reform is an instance of its policy. Like the Canadian imperialists,[24] the Unionist Party focuses on small agricultural landholders as the base for an egalitarian society, and it supports the maintenance of the Empire. The State Labour Party in the novel is in favour of a quicker and more drastic redistribution of wealth: "a state-made millennium" (91) of nationalized business. The disadvantages of both positions are also clear in the novel. Percy Acourt, the shining light of the Unionists, is cold and unfeeling, and has the tendency to become too abstract and speculative; his friendship with Pamela supplies "that touch of human sympathy which it was his defect to be without" (102). The Gommies,[25] organizers for the Labour Party, are extremists, wholly unimaginative, "fierce, pale, uncompromising slaves of the single idea" (47). Clearly, as Pamela suggests, neither side has all the truth. Both she and her stepmother fulfill a necessary function when they point the way to a kind of political reform that operates beyond party lines.

The choice of political affiliation is to some extent determined by personal considerations in *The Consort*, as Thomas Tausky has noted.[26] Pargeter forsakes the Unionists for Labour in order to preserve an area of mind "different from his wife's" (73). Pamela leaves the Unionists to canvass for her father out of filial duty and a desire to support his independence from her stepmother. Mary moves from left to centre under the tutelage of Acourt, the young Tory for whom she cherishes an unacknowledged love. But while Pargeter's only motive is opposition to his wife, Pamela's and Mary's motives are also ideological. Mary grew up in a liberal household, but saw the Liberal Party change from support of social legislation to support for unrestrained capitalism. "Old Lord Lossel, her father, had outlived, as it were, his political convictions, and had gone on balloting in the Liberal faith long after his vote had begun to promote something quite different" (47). Raised to regard her inheritance as a public trust, Mary carries on her father's principles by switching to the Labour Party, and she becomes well known for her generosity to public causes; she is regarded as a useful example to other millionaires by the Labour organizers, Clarence and Esther Gommie. But she realizes that "the world of the mind is alive and forever changing" (62) and that her party affiliation must be discarded when outgrown. She decides to support a conservative scheme for financing the purchase of land by small farmers and so signals her change of party. Her move to the conservative Unionist Party is not simply a slavish attempt to gain the love of Acourt; it is an attempt to embody her instinct for social progress in a new reality. Similarly, Pamela discovers a need to blend her party principles with a knowledge of the social reality that the Labour Party seems to represent. When she begins campaigning for her father, she finds little to admire in the socialist cause: "I wish I could believe in State-made millenniums, but I can't. And I wish I loved and panted for humanity in its cruder aspects, but I don't. And I wish I could see qualities in the British working-classes to make me want them to control my affairs, and those of the country, but I haven't discovered them yet, and I don't believe anybody else has" (91).

Yet Pamela remains open to change. She tells Acourt that she cannot believe that "all the sophisms can be on one side and all the truth on the other" (106). Canvassing in the working-class districts of High Pollard exposes Pamela to a poverty both physical and emotional which her party platform does not take into account. She meets a poor woman in a lean-to kitchen who is attempting to prepare her husband's meagre dinner while politely fending off two political canvassers and a funeral-subscription collector; she is rebuffed on a suburban doorstep by an elderly woman who abruptly tells her, "We've got death. And the funeral's in the afternoon" (243). Such experiences shake her political faith; while "her mind would never be won either to the proposals or the methods of Socialism ... her heart shook before her new vision of its claim" (189). Her knowledge of the working class brings her to an understanding of class that goes beyond mere pity: "How long will they endure it? Must we have a revolution to teach us to respect the decencies of life?" (243). When she encounters Acourt near the end of the campaign, she can state clearly what she has learned from canvassing in the socialist cause: "It has taught me to suspect selfishness even in some of our own ideals, and – that there is no work in the world that should tempt us before the lifting up of our own" (245). Pamela's implicit criticism of conservative economic and imperial policy, while it does not tempt her to throw aside her party loyalties, does allow her to look beyond the limits of party, as her stepmother Mary does. The book supports Pamela's recognition of consciousness beyond party; when she and Acourt inherit the administration of Mary's trust fund, they are given an opportunity to work for social change outside the strictures of the party system.

The narrator of the novel shows her sympathy with the working class in her picture of Pamela's conversion. But the narrator has little hope that the democratic system will solve society's ills. "The people" (as Lady Flora Bellamy styles them) have no ability to see their own long-term good. They are more interested in simply asserting their new-found power. Pamela voices an account of the workings of politics in general which the narrator does not contradict: "The strong have always taken what they could lay their hands on. The balance of strength has shifted. That's all. It used to be the man with the arm, now it's the man with the vote" (92). On the evening of Leland Pargeter's defeat, a Liberal government is elected with enormous popular support. The narrator attempts to put the victory into historical context, alluding to the general swell of democratic reform following the Liberal victory of 1906, including the People's Budget and the Parliament Bill of 1910:

It was one of the early years of active democratic sway in England, when power and opportunity were suddenly realised to the full, and the idea still reigned among the people of how most signally to assert themselves. Privilege had begun to go down like the poor images of a cult under a horde of hammers. It was already long since persons attached to the old regime had comforted themselves with the assurance that the people loved a lord, long since that affection had been proved abstract and social, and by no means cherished to the point of fatuity. The task of depriving the barons of their political entity was fully accomplished in that year; the peer in the arena was henceforth to figure, so to speak, in his shirt-sleeves. Majesty remained, deeper rooted in the hearts of the people; but its levees and drawing rooms were at once less and more popular; the roots required and obtained assiduous watering ... Socialistic taxation reached that year its most alluring aspect ... It was a record year for the emigration of the upper middle-classes, the year that marked for later history, more definitely than any other, the great drift away that left the island the beloved but embarrassing responsibility to the race that elderly relatives so often become. (302–3)

If the tone of the passage is "embittered,"[27] as Thomas Tausky suggests, it is not hopeless. The narrator maintains the two positive values that are upheld throughout Duncan's portrayal of social change: the future of colonies and affection for the monarch. Indeed, as Tausky suggests, the assessment of Britain and the colonies, including Canada, remains identical to that in *The Imperialist*; Duncan maintains the colonial perspective that sees Canada's blending of democracy and monarchy, her class system of "all hard-working folk together" (*Imp.*, 47), as an ideal to be striven for.

For Duncan, "the only democracy which, so far as we know, is a practical working success"[28] is the afterlife. Human selfishness, in its political manifestation as modern democracy, allows personal and party ambition to prevent the governing of society by human compassion and British ideals. While *The Imperialist* and *The Burnt Offering* end on a hopeful note of reaching towards the ideals of country and monarch, the general inability to overcome self-interest defeats the reforms of John Church and forces Pamela Pargeter to work outside the political system.

CHAPTER SIX

Nation and Empire: Growing Goldenrod in Simla

> It is the King's goldenrod ... and I gathered the
> seed one splendid autumn afternoon in Canada;
> so here on the shelf it may claim its humble part
> in the Imperial idea.
>
> *On the Other Side of the Latch*

Sara Jeannette Duncan was naturally interested in the composition and the future of the British Empire.[1] She grew up at a time when the future of Canada and its status within the Empire were topics of debate in local newspapers, in the House of Commons, and in literature. At the age of thirty she became part of the Anglo-Indian community and witnessed the rise of the Indian Nationalist movement and a bitter debate in England over colonial policy in India. Her interest in nationality, kindled by her life in Canada and her own status as a colonial, led her to realize the necessity of practical independence in everyday affairs for colonial countries; yet her belief in the British heritage and the natural cohesiveness of the English-speaking community ("the Anglo-Saxon race") led her to hope for the eventual overcoming of national barriers. Her garden of goldenrod, grown on a "shelf" jutting out from the mountainside in Simla from seed gathered in Canada, provides a fitting metaphor for Duncan's transplanting of her "colonial perspective" from its Canadian roots to an Indian flowering.

The Empire was the actual political mechanism that functionally united the "Anglo-Saxon race" (except for the United States); yet its focus of power in England tended to stifle its member countries' legitimate aspirations toward nationhood. The Empire had proved an unwieldy and inflexible system of government for Canada, where local considerations were often lost in Britain's drive for rapprochement with the United States (in the Alaska Panhandle dispute, for example). It had also been a problem in India, where the long delay in communications with the Colonial Office as well as the unfamiliarity of British politicians with Indian culture had caused gaffes of monumental proportions. As Duncan wrote in 1896: "In dealing with imperial problems, the empire has a great and deplorable tendency to overlook or to minimize local knowledge and local desires. We have too many instances of this in India to forget it for a moment. Certain broad lines of policy are marked out, and if remote colonial interests happen to fall in with them, well and good; if not, so much the worse for the colonials."² Yet the British Empire and its "civilizing mission" constituted the beginning of the peaceful federation of mankind to which Duncan looked forward; she saw loyalty to the crown and ties of familial sentiment uniting countries with diverse cultures in peaceful trade and military co-operation. The various alternatives proposed for reforming the Empire and the dissection of its actual workings are major themes in her novels.

Duncan's Canadian political and intellectual perspective led her to see the Empire's potential to reconcile universal ideals with local realities. Her framework of "popular idealism," which considered real local conditions to be variable manifestations of ideal truth, allowed her to view the Empire as a group of fairly independent countries united by the ideal of loyalty. Like the Canadian members of the Imperial Federation movement, she supported the Empire as a focus of moral stability against the scepticism and moral relativism that accompanied modern utilitarian materialism.³ But she did not support the Imperial Federation movement uncritically in her novels; while she agreed with its ideals, which she felt held the Empire together, she also depicted the attempt to codify such ideals in the diverse circumstances of many countries as apt to lead to injustice and inflexibility. As a colonial herself, she is sceptical in *The Imperialist* of plans that would allow the English a permanent vote on colonial matters; as an Anglo-Indian, she portrays the inflexible application of principles drawn from the imperial centre as essentially destructive in *His Honor, and a Lady* and *Set In Authority*. Instead of a uniform Empire, Duncan portrays a united Empire held together by bonds of sentiment, whose member states share the common desire to embody the ideals of their British heritage in real life.

The metaphor of the "family" of Empire, in which Canada was the brilliant and beautiful daughter, led Duncan to portray a special role for women in the maintenance of Empire. By becoming a "memsahib like another," Helen Browne of *The Simple Adventures of a Memsahib* constitutes a living link between her little bit of India and the small town of Canbury where her parents and sisters still reside; they are forever concerned about the future of India, and the future of Empire, because Helen is there. Duncan states that, for Canbury, "feminine connections" with the colonies through intermarriage and immigration are the only ones that are really binding; each of the love stories in the novels represents not only a cementing of the relationship between the two countries but also a tangible alternative to the abstract political ties that the male characters negotiate.

The maintenance of such bonds are traditionally women's work in the nuclear family. The supposed triumph of emotion, of the heart, in feminine nature gives women the role of peacemaker. Duncan's vision of a feminine Canada (or Anglo-India) who creates and maintains ties with England and finds her life's work and independence through the maintenance of that relationship is thus a doubly colonial vision – one drawn from Duncan's Canadian intellectual roots and modified by her "femininity" as created under patriarchy.

THE AMOUNT of contemporary literature on the subject of the Empire and proposals for imperial federation is overwhelming, as Dr Henry discovers in *The Imperialist* when he decides to research the topic. He read "the Manchester school to begin with – sat out on the verandah reading Cobden and Bright the whole summer … He thought they talked an awful lot of sense, those fellows from the English point of view. 'D'ye mean to tell me,' he'd say, 'that a generation born and bred in political doctrine of that sort is going to hold on to the colonies at a sacrifice? They'd rather let 'em go at a sacrifice!' Well, then he got to reading the other side of the question, and old Ormiston lent him Parkin, and he lent old Ormiston Goldwin Smith, and then he subscribed to the *Times* for six months" (200). As Dr Henry discovers, the Canadian imperialist view of the British Empire was formed within a debate that started in England in the early nineteenth century. The two sides in the debate, the Manchester School (so called because they spoke for the manufacturing interests based in Manchester) and the Imperial Federationists, both focused on the future good of England, but they had different views on how to secure that good.

It was popular economic wisdom that colonies were necessary to England's economic health; they produced raw materials for the manufacturing sector, they bought manufactured goods, and they were necessary counters in the periodic wars between European powers. But the American War of Independence in 1776 had sparked a controversy in Britain over the necessity of maintaining colonies at all. Britain had exercised force against her own people in order to keep the United States in the Empire; many felt that no moral or political justification for that force existed. The debate continued with the increasing participation of the British government in the affairs of India. In response, Edmund Burke enunciated the principle by which conservatives justified government of the Empire, that authority over a subject people "ought to be some way or other exercised ultimately for their benefit."[4]

For the "settlement" colonies such as Canada and Australia, which could be held by "the plough" of British agricultural colonists, the benefit of the imperial connection was obvious to British Imperialists; such colonies had gained British government and institutions and the force of the British navy in settling their local disputes. In return, Britain gained military allies, markets for manufactured goods, and the possibility of peaceful social reform through emigration. The settlement colonies could assist the poor in England through freer trade in agricultural products and through emigration of honest working people to farms in the colonies. The settlers, small landholders, seemed able to preserve the traditional values of independence and a cohesive family life; their work seemed physically and mentally healthy (as opposed to equivalent labour in the industrial work force). Agriculture appeared to foster friendly relations between classes rather than clashes between combinations and labour unions. These characteristics fostered a renewal of humankind that Duncan, along with Canadian thinkers such as G.T. Dennison, felt would lead to a full and more peaceful life. A healthy agricultural base provided a stable market and promoted the growth of small manufacturing.

Duncan dramatizes the possibilities of imperial agriculture as the basis of renewal of British society. She twice mentions a scheme for land redistribution that would increase the number of small landholders and reduce the number of unemployed industrial labourers: Mary Pargeter in *The Consort* finances such a scheme, and John Game in *The Burnt Offering* approves of a similar plan for India. For Duncan, however, the settlement colonies provide the real focus for social reform based on agriculture. She sees Canada as a sort of escape valve for Britons who are discouraged by the direction that their country is taking under democratic government. When the Unionist Party is turned out in *The Consort*, Canada profits "incalculably from the money tide that set steadily across the Atlantic" (303), and emigration to Canada reaches a record high. In *The Imperialist*, most emigrants from Britain find a "difficult kind of prosperity" (73) which is, nonetheless, better than what they could have expected at home; free schooling and the democratic impulse have broken down class barriers and created a society of "hard-working folk together" (47). The opportunity that the colonies and, especially, Canada offer has allowed characters in *The Imperialist* and *Cousin Cinderella* to better their lot. Lorne's father John Murchison, an emigrant from Scotland, has built his small hardware business into a distribution house for the products of his own foundry by serving the needs of the local agricultural population; the noise from the foundry, which "finicking visitors to Elgin found ... wearing," indicates to John Murchison "the music that honours the conqueror of circumstances" (*Imp.*, 24). Senator Trent of *Cousin Cinderella* has founded a town, made a fortune in the lumber business, and been honoured by his government. In both novels, Canada is presented as an escape from incarceration in England. Mary Trent describes why her father will never return to England: "He adopted Canada forty years ago in the most specific kind of way; and I believe he feels that to go back again even for a visit would be to admit that for him the bargain wasn't perfectly ideal. As a matter of fact, it has been ideal ... People do seem to escape like that from the British Isles; I've noticed other cases. With quite a pleasant sentiment about their early cells, and great affection for the warder, they simply don't want to set foot there again" (8–9). Lorne's fellow delegates in England congratulate each other on having decided to emigrate and speak with horror of the crowded, uncomfortable conditions of England.

But in the colonies in Egypt, Africa, India, Burma, and New Zealand, which could only be held by "the sword" of British military might, the benefits of maintaining the Empire seemed less obvious; the expenditures for military defence appeared unjustified by the resulting tax and trade revenue, and shows of military force did not always get governments re-elected. Anthony Andover

Thame, the fictional viceroy in Duncan's *Set in Authority*, discusses the problems of rule by military might in an unpublished manuscript written before he goes out to India; his fiancée states that "he practically repudiates all that we hold by the sword, and confines us, in the world, to the parts we can plough" (14), an attitude that changes rather quickly after he takes office. The experience of "lifting up" the mass of India, the actual experience of rule which was supposed to be for the good of others, Duncan and her contemporaries argued, often convinced waverers of the importance of the British mission in India. Burke's principle of force wielded for the good of the governed became the justification for the "Imperial Idea," the "white man's burden" of Rudyard Kipling.

The Imperial Idea of the late-Victorian era was, in essence, a belief in a moral justification for the exercise of British military power against indigenous groups of "blacks." Part of that justification was certainly the racist belief in the superiority of the British, but it was also partly a belief that the Empire would be a prelude to a federation of mankind. In his study of Anglo-Indian literature, Shamsul Islam suggests that imperial ideologies have always included a positive belief in internationalism and the preservation of peace: "The root idea of empire in ancient and medieval days was that of a federation of states, under a universal law and a hegemony, covering the entire known world; it was based on a philosophy of peace, order, discipline and internationalism. Till the turn of the present century, imperialism was seen by many, particularly the Europeans, in more or less similar terms, especially as a civilizing mission."[5] The exercise of force in support of the ideal of unity and peace was held to be justified, part of an ethic of service to the human race. Thomas Carlyle's call to quit self-questioning and instead "work thou in well-doing" was interpreted by the Victorians as the task of bringing the light of British justice, order, and Christian religion to the seemingly dark areas of the world.

Duncan was concerned about the consequences of sacrificial service to colonies that could only be held by British military might, and which were unsuited to colonization by British settlers. The colonies of Canada, Australia, New Zealand, and other temperate climates encouraged the transfer of allegiance to the new country, but the stifling climate, the dangers to health, and the "unsympathetic masses" of the local population discouraged such a transfer in India: "The colonial takes root in his New Zealand, in his Canada. He acquires permanent interests, unknown to our own shifting community ... The men of permanent interests must consider ultimate effects, the transient money-maker of ten or twenty years can afford to ignore them."[6] Anglo-Indians for the most part were not interested in local affairs; they could not feel at home in India because the climate and the country made them ill. For the most part, they educated their children "at Home," and so were separated from them for long periods; wives and single women sent out to keep house for relatives spent months in making repeated trips between family members in England and India. Such transitory devotion to India led to exploitation – financial among the merchants and political among the civilian "secretaries" and government appointees – rather than the "civilizing" mission of Empire. But it also led to an increasing zeal on the part of Anglo-Indians to defend what they thought of as the best interests of India against the party politics of home government appointees. To the extent that Duncan adopted that Anglo-Indian point of view, she remained a colonial in India.

Like her imperialist contemporaries, Duncan believed that the moral argument of the Imperial Idea of social reform, plus the advantage of having military bases in many parts of the world and a secure market for British manufactured goods in the colonies, were important arguments for the maintenance and strengthening of the Empire. But the Liberals and Labour pointed out that the actual practice of British authority contradicted the notion that British rule worked to help subject peoples, and so they argued that the Empire had no moral justification. More important, thinkers such as Richard Cobden and John Bright of the Manchester School noted that the colonies cost more money than they brought in; that colonies expected military protection but refused to pay for it or to allow the British to govern in return; that increased trade with the Americans since the "revolution" proved that independent former colonies would be better customers outside the Empire.[7] Liberals opposed the active foreign policy supporting British interests in Europe and the Middle East introduced by Disraeli, and argued that Britain had no right to interfere in other nations' affairs. In Canada, Duncan's friend and former employer Goldwin Smith identified himself with the Manchester School and argued in *Canada and the Canadian Question* that both Britain and Canada would be better off if Canada joined the United States.

The depression of the 1880s raised the possibility that without colonies (whether held by the plough or the sword) or active foreign intervention in the colony-making of other European nations, Britain could shrink into a "third-rate isle." The Imperial Federation League proposed an imperial *zollverein*, like the one started by the Germans to alleviate the depression, that would revive the ideal of service to less "advanced" peoples and link it to the promotion of British "prestige" in international affairs.

Canadians were similarly divided between imperialist and Manchester School ideas. While Sir John A. Macdonald declared, "A British subject I was born, a British subject I will die," he also introduced the National Policy, which discriminated against British manufacturers.[8] Some supported Smith's call to join the United States, or the Liberals' policy of economic union. Even Canadian imperialists had difficulty reconciling the rhetoric of imperialism with Britain's practice of sacrificing Canadian affairs to placate the United States. Some Canadians felt that their loyalty, so important to the imperialists, meant nothing to the British government, and they began to identify the Empire with British tradition and the Anglo-Saxon race rather than with Britain itself. Robert Grant Haliburton, one of the original members of the Canada First movement, provides a typical illustration of this shift in the rationale for Imperial Federation. In his pamphlet on the Treaty of Washington (published in 1872), he condemns the British for their "utter selfishness" in negotiating away Canadian fishing rights in order to settle their own problems with the US. The British have governed the Empire on "the principle of self-interest," he states, and so have squandered the real basis of Empire, the ideal of loyalty to the Crown. However, despite his bitter denunciation of the treatment of Canada by the British, he does not advocate Canadian independence; he proposes, instead, that Canadians learn from the British betrayal, and reunite the Empire in the teeth of those Britons who have dismantled it: "The pole-star of the United Empire Loyalists of 1776 was loyalty to the Crown, and it led them, as we have seen, to disunion, to exile, to sacrifices, to humiliation. The watchword of the United Empire Loyalists of the future must be, 'Reunion of the Empire' and 'Loyalty to the Race.'"[9] In this remarkably bitter document, published in England and Canada, Haliburton essentially disavows any Canadian subservience to Britain while still advocating a united Empire. For Haliburton and other imperial federationists, the preservation of the Empire was a stable value, an assumed norm, which was wholly compatible with practical colonial independence.[10]

Imperialists in Canada, the US, and Britain interpreted the debate about the future of the Empire in terms of the opposition of monetary self-interest and sacrificial loyalty. They found the emphasis of the Manchester School thinkers upon the monetary value (or burden) of colonies to be morally self-condemning. The enemies of Empire, the middle-class philistines of Matthew Arnold's *Culture and Anarchy*, seemed to value money over the traditions of loyalty, peace, monarchy, liberty, and altruism. Imperialists in Canada, the US, and Britain "were at one in their search for values, both personal and political, which would check the spirit of commercialism and the social atomization of their time."[11]

Duncan's particular understanding of idealism is the context in which she dramatizes her ideas about the Empire. Like Haliburton, she locates the value of the Empire in the ideals of "the race" and in the heritage of British institutions, rather than in Britain itself. "The ideals of British government," upon which Lorne Murchison bases his appeal to the people of Elgin, form the heritage of the British colonies: "British statesmen could bring us nothing better than the ideals of British government ... That precious cargo was our heritage, and we never threw it overboard" (*Imp.*, 230). Love for and understanding of ideals such as liberty, altruism, loyalty, and justice are inherent in members of "the race": "The Empire is summed up in the race, and the flag flies for its ideals" (*Imp.*, 216). However, Duncan locates the ideals of the Empire in the "human product" of British culture, the heroic individual who is able to see beyond self-interest and the narrow application of formulas towards the final end of mutual help and trust among peoples.

For Duncan, loyalty to the monarch, who was supposed to embody the community of British peoples and the abstract ideals that have resulted from the evolutionary process of British history, summed up the Empire. While "the first principle of democracy is essentially selfish," loyalty to the monarch is representative of the beauty of self-sacrifice in a materialistic age: "Are we not losing something in the rapid progress of the theory that formulates itself in 'Every man for himself, and the devil take royalty'? It is excellent common sense; but in its evolution has not an impalpable essence escaped us that is more beautiful, if not more profitable, than common sense? I cannot think of any nobler virtue than that by which a man lays down his life for his king, and counts it as nothing, blind, ignorant, unreasoning as it is."[12] Duncan specifically opposes loyalty to common sense; she even prefers ignorance and unreason to the kind of sensibility that constantly weighs and measures before considering action. Self-sacrifice in the service of the monarch, as a spontaneous, heartfelt action, is the basis of the Empire.

For the British in India, loyalty is transferred to the figure of the viceroy, who embodies the Imperial Idea of sacrifice in the service of making a better world; loyalty to him as a person is the human equivalent of their loyalty and submission to the Idea.

Whatever happens elsewhere in these days of triumphant democracies, in India the Ruler survives. He is the shadow of the King, but the substance of kingship is curiously and pathetically his; and his sovereignty is most real with those who again represent him ... in lonely places which the Viceroy's foot never presses and his eye never sees, men of his own race find in his person the authority for the purpose of their whole lives. He is the judge of all they do and the symbol by which they do it. Reward and censure are in his hand and he stands for whatever there is in the task of men that is sweeter than praise and more bitter than blame. He stands for the idea, the scheme and the intention to which they are all pledged; and through the long sacrifice of the arid years something of their loyalty and devotion and submission to the idea gathers in the human way about the sign of it. (SA, 32–3)

Thus loyalty becomes the human equivalent of the dedication to ideals that the popular mind associated with the British Empire. In rural Elgin, in The Imperialist, "a sentiment of affection for the reigning house" (58) prevails and, even though that sentiment is "arbitrary, rococo" (58), it becomes the focus for the love of motherland which lifts the minds of the first- and second-generation immigrants of the Canadian town up from material considerations towards the larger consideration of the future of their nation. Similarly, in The Burnt Offering, the viceroy seems to symbolize the ideal of peace and order against the chaos created by nationalist agitation; the appearance of the viceroy after a terrorist attack forms

the basis for a new reconciliation between the British government
and the people in India.

Duncan's heroes express the self-sacrifice that loyalty to the monarch symbolizes by sacrificing their own peace of mind and, in
some cases, their lives to make the world a better place. In *The
Burnt Offering*, Michael Foley enunciates this principle clearly when
he says that he is attempting to bring "justice and peace, and
freedom and that sort of thing" (60) to India, despite homesickness
and illness. Lorne Murchison, who sacrifices his political career,
and John Game, who is eventually assassinated, are other hero
figures. Like Murchison and Game, those who attempt to impose
their own version of civilization are often thwarted by local conditions in Duncan's novels. Yet notions of helping Indians through
legislation, education, and example persist among Duncan's Anglo-
Indian characters. The direction such impulses should take is often
disputed: John Church wonders whether English education is helping or hindering Indians in *His Honor, and a Lady*, and Joan Mills
and John Game (in *The Burnt Offering*) dispute whether continued
English government will produce the desired outcome of peaceful,
prosperous life for the Indian populace. But the Imperial Idea of
rendering service to the "less-advanced" nations of the world
remains the focus of the Indian novels.

WHILE CANADIAN AND BRITISH IMPERIALISTS shared the belief
that the preservation of the Empire was the preservation of a concept of ideal value in the face of materialism, they differed on how
that value could be embodied in a practical policy that would
promote their goals. Imperialists from various nations all saw the
Empire from a point of view dictated by national interests. Canadian imperialism was essentially a strategy for Canadian nationalism, as Carl Berger has demonstrated,[13] and many Canadian
imperialists were vocal in asserting Canadian interests in a possible
federation. Canadians felt that Canada had a better chance of
withstanding the commercial and military aggressiveness of the
United States by balancing its powerful neighbour against the imperial power of England. The Imperial Federation movement, whose
greatest spokesman was the Canadian George Parkin, was a
response to the desire of colonials and some Britons to allow colonies to remain within the Empire and yet exercise some control

over their own foreign policy; the reorganization of the Empire along federal lines, including some kind of imperial representative parliament, seemed to guarantee the strength of the British connection to ward off the influence of the US, as well as allowing Canada a voice in her own affairs. Canadians envisioned the Empire evolving into a federation of independent states, with a common foreign and trade policy made by a council with elected representatives from all the member states. Such a federation, they felt, would be centred in, if not dominated by, Canada, as the eldest and most developed of the colonies and the originator of the idea of the federated Empire. Canadians felt that they, rather than Britons, had the expertise and material wealth necessary to guide the Empire in the coming years of decline for England as an international power.[14]

The reception of imperial federation in a prosperous town in Canada is the focus of Duncan's one novel set in Canada – *The Imperialist*.[15] Canada's status within the Empire becomes part of Lorne Murchison's election campaign when the Liberal Party adopts the scheme of imperial preference trade, put forward by the British politician Wallingham (probably based on Joseph Chamberlain) as its platform. The Liberal Party proposes that English goods be let into Canada "free, or cheap" (136) in return for the lowering of tariffs on Canadian agricultural products in England. The great debate over imperial preference trade is essentially a debate between the head and the heart. The allegiance to the throne is resident in the heart (22); Lorne's "eager apprehending heart" (226) is the force that carries him away from his set text in his final election speech. Lorne sees much more than economic benefit in increased ties with Britain: "You would think, to read the papers, that all its merits could be put into dollars and cents" (137), he complains. Lorne believes that the "moral aspect" (137) of British influence on the evolution of Canada will help to develop Canadian personality: "We're all right out here, but we're young and thin and weedy. They didn't grow so fast in England, to begin with, and now they're rich with character and strong with conduct and hoary with ideals ... They've developed the finest human product there is, the cleanest, the most disinterested, and we want to keep up the relationship – it's important" (98). The debate between "dollars and cents" and "the moral aspect" in the minds of Elgin residents is exemplified in John Murchison, whose sceptical support for the Empire is the middle position between Lorne and the Conservatives. John likes the idea of placing political honour and public devotion, ideals he associates with England, above material considerations. He associates imperial federation with a knightly code of honour,[16] bringing up echoes of Tennyson's Arthur and the modern battle for stability and the triumph of good he represented for Victorian readers. Even so, John is aware of the "practical difficulties" that Lorne's scheme would present to Elgin.

Imperial preference trade, as Lorne describes it, is not a wholly impractical idea. Lorne sees the farmers of Fox County as the basis for the community of Elgin itself; John Murchison's retail business, the factory owned by Milburn, and the manufacturing classes in general depend upon the prosperity of the farmers, who are the closest market for their goods. The National Policy of the Conservative government, according to the narrator, "divided the industrial and the agricultural interests" (167) by favouring the former at the expense of the latter. Imperial preference would restore more natural relations between industry and agriculture by providing a guaranteed market for agricultural goods; the newly prosperous farmers would buy enough to make up for the competition of British manufacturers.

John Murchison clearly sees the possible advantage to his business in imperial preference. Though he realizes that he may suffer a short-term loss, he believes that loss will be made up in the general prosperity of the country: "He said he was more concerned to see big prices in British markets for Canadian crops than he was to put big prices on ironware he couldn't sell. He was more afraid of hard times among the farmers of Canada than he was of competition by the manufacturers of England" (206). He agrees with Lorne that the British manufacturer will have trouble competing with local industries in Canada: "The British manufacturer can't possibly get the better of men on the spot, who know to a nut the local requirements" (173). Imperial preference, as Lorne presents it, benefits the country by benefitting the farmers; the farmers respond by favouring Lorne's candidacy (207).

Businessmen who, like John Murchison, are capable of responding to the ideals that the Empire represents, and who have little worry for their own material prosperity under the scheme, are able to support Lorne even though his youthful enthusiasm carries him away. The manufacturers, who see no further than the short term, unite against imperial preference. Octavius Milburn, the philistine "representative man" of the novel,[17] puts forth the view of his kind: "The Empire looks nice on the map, but when it comes to practical politics their bread and butter's in the home industries. There's a great principle at stake ... Liberals ... may talk big, but when it comes to the ballot-box you'll have the whole manufacturing interest of the place behind you, and nobody the wiser. It's a great thing to carry the standard on an issue above and beyond party politics – it's purer air" (166). Duncan uses the rhetoric of the idealists ironically to condemn Milburn. Speaking only from self-interest, he congratulates his Conservative ally for being able to stand up for the principle of profit, at no possible risk to himself.

Suspicion of British conduct in the actual arrangements of imperial preference is another major factor mitigating Elgin's support for Lorne's candidacy. Quite simply, Elgin residents believe that they have learned from history that the British cannot be trusted to live by their own ideals. "Great Britain had sold them before, and she would sell them again" (210) is a common reaction in Elgin. Even the farmers, who would benefit most directly from the scheme, are suspicious: "Those of Fox County thought it looked very well, but it was pretty sure to work out some other way" (149).

Lorne is not elected, and imperial preference fails in England as well; but what Lorne fails to achieve politically, the women in the novel succeed in doing by methods totally outside the political system. The triumph of the heart in maintaining close sentimental ties between Canada and Britain is achieved by marriages which are not simply symbolic of the political theme but offer a practical alternative to it. The ideals of Hugh Finlay are successfully integrated into Canadian society by the active intervention of Advena Murchison's love and Dr Drummond's common sense, which overcome Hugh's allegiance to his old-world values. A tangible alliance between Canada and Britain is created in their marriage, a kind of alliance which Duncan suggests is, finally, much more effective than a mere piece of legislation, because it literally ties Canadians to Britons as family members. Similarly, Dr Drummond's commitment to Canada will guide Christie Cameron's adaptation to her new home yet maintain connection with the old, and even Dora Milburn's marriage, though clearly an alliance between shallow and hypocritical individuals, will add to the bonds of existing sentiment between the two countries.

Similarly, Mary Trent comes to understand how a woman's traditional role within a nuclear family can work as a force for political
unity within the family of the Empire while she is on a visit to
England in *Cousin Cinderella*. Up until that time, Mary has experienced life as a child, a daughter, and a sister; in England she
takes upon herself the role of independent actor in international
politics. Like Canada, Mary has ordinarily felt herself to have little
identity beyond that given her by her parental association and
material wealth. But in London, Mary's view of herself and her
country changes. She is invited to become a naturalized British
citizen by allowing herself to be moulded by British social standards; she learns that she, like Canada, can exert power to bring
about desirable changes. Mary discovers her Canadian identity
together with her personal role in life; she fulfills both when she
marries Lord Peter Doleford, the "prince charming" implied by the
title.

Mary Trent discovers her power to act autonomously in a moment
of extraordinary clarity. Riding in Mrs Jarvis's electric car, she realizes that she is being offered a role in the trans-Atlantic drama of
alliances. Mrs Jarvis has a son, Billy Milliken, whom she would
like to settle in life; Mary and her money seem to be the ideal
anchor for the empty-headed Billy. Mary realizes that she has something that London wants; she loses her awe of London, and gains
a sense of independence:

It is the kind of thing one is ashamed to write, but I must confess that I
drew from Mrs. Jarvis at this moment the definite thrill of a new per-
ception, something captivating and delicious. Suddenly, without Graham,
without anybody, moving through the lovely, thronged, wet, lamplit London streets in Mrs. Jarvis' electric brougham, I felt myself realised –
realised in London, not only by the person who happened to be near me,
but in a vague, delightful, potential sense by London. Realised, not a bit
for what I was – that wouldn't, I am afraid, have carried me very far –
nor exactly for what I represented, but for something else, for what I
might, under favourable circumstances, be made to represent. (126)

Mary's moment of self-discovery is not egotistical – she does not
feel that her essence has been recognized and rewarded but, rather,
that her independence has been granted. Her dowry allows her to
dictate the terms of a marriage, and the "solicitation" of London

makes her realize that she, like Canada, can use her wealth for a purpose. Her mere existence, as a woman with a dowry, gives her the power to act. From her new perspective, Mary feels a "divine disdain of London" (127) and the sense that she has the power to make a choice, once and for all, whether or not she wants to be just a colonial, whether she wants to become a Briton.

Mary becomes an agent of union between Canada and Britain by marrying Doleford and bringing her dowry to the rescue of the ancient Pavisay family. The marriage proposed earlier in the novel, between Doleford's sister Barbara and Mary's brother Graham, is clearly inappropriate; Graham would lose the inheritance of independence (310) due to him both as a Canadian and as a man. Mary, as a woman adept in the maintenance of sentiment between family members (even large families like the British Empire) and "more or less born into a state of bondage" (310), is the logical choice to preserve the ties of Empire through marriage. As Doleford remarks, "In our dealings with the colonies, the heart is supposed to have more of a chance" (362). Mary's alliance with Doleford promises that Canada's independence, as well as her ties with England, will be preserved.

The balance between imperial ties and national self-interest is also a focus for the depiction of the relations of Empire in two novels set in India. In *The Burnt Offering* and *Set In Authority*, Vulcan Mills and Lord Thame, respectively, attempt to apply abstract ideas drawn from their British experience to India, making absolutely no allowance for local circumstances. The emphasis in the novels is on the equal application of the law throughout the Empire, a strategy that was central to the Utilitarian vision of the government of India; social-justice legislation, higher education, and adherence to the principles of British justice were supposed to create a renewed, civilized society. But, as so often noted, few of the Utilitarian writers on India actually went there; in Duncan's novels, the followers of Utilitarianism, Vulcan Mills and Viceroy Thame, form their ideas about India in abstraction and then try to transplant them to a reality that baffles them. In both cases, the male characters ignore or misunderstand the alternative vision for political action offered by the women in the novel; Mills misunderstands his daughter's engagement to Bepin Behari Dey and Thame misunderstands the women who offer him assistance. Rather than working within the limits of the physical and the personal, Mills and

Thame attempt to apply the asbstract values of the centre without change and, not surprisingly, they fail.

In *The Burnt Offering*, Vulcan Mills applies his socialist standard of liberty and equality without regard to its actual effects among Indians. Mills represents the British Liberal and Labour opposition to all limitation of political rights and all exercise of British force in India, and their call for a withdrawal of troops. He refuses to modify his views to take account of the new information available to him in India, or even to suit the changing policy of his party: "He tramped after his ideal wherever he saw it, tramped after it in the same old heavy boots" (126). Opposing Mills in *The Burnt Offering* are Michael Foley and his friend John Game; they too express the Imperial Idea through their defence of the ideal of British liberty, which they interpret as free political debate in a stable society. But from their colonial perspective, the India of *The Burnt Offering* is far from stable, and political freedom must be circumscribed by reasonable limits. Foley and Game allow Ganendra Thakore to continue his program of publications and speechmaking, despite his suspected association with political violence. The narrator states that their respect for political freedom is misunderstood by India as weakness or folly, yet Game and Foley maintain the principles of British freedom until what seems to be the last possible moment. When they finally pass a law designed to allow them to arrest Thakore, the British-educated opposition quotes "Mill on liberty and Shakespeare on the human heart" (98), but Indian society proves its inability to understand the substance of their authorities by wondering "at the leniency that left her dangerous leader abroad so long" (97–8). Unlike Mills, Game and his colleagues temper the application of British principles with practical knowledge of Indian circumstances.

Duncan's depiction of imperial British justice in *Set in Authority* also makes a powerful case for the necessity of considering local variations when determining exactly how those principles should be applied; the book also makes a case for the power of women to interpret sensitive political situations. In *Set In Authority*, Henry Morgan (the disguised Herbert Tring) has been charged with the murder of "a native"; he is tried, against the opposition of most of the British population, by Sir Ahmet Hossein, a "native" judge. The circumstances of the murder are confused, but Hossein attempts to serve justice by relying on his integrity and instincts. He accepts the jury's guilty verdict on the charge of culpable homicide and imposes a surprisingly light sentence of two years' imprisonment; he feels that his sentence will satisfy those British who object to "natives" in positions of judicial power, yet pacify those Indians who feel that the justice system is biased against them. But the viceroy, a man noted for his inflexible application of the principle of absolute equality between British and Indian subjects, attempts to re-open the case in order to secure a more severe punishment.[18]

Eliot Arden, the chief commissioner in the area where the crime took place, opposes the government appeal. His local point of view allows him to see that British traditions of evidence and objective justice cannot work unimpeded in a country with no such tradition, and his intimate knowledge of the local people leads him to suspect that much of the new evidence for the appeal was manufactured in response to the viceroy's appeal. He explains his view of the case: "I think justice carried rather obliquely. I think culpable homicide, on the evidence, was the right verdict, and not murder; I also think Morgan should have got a good deal more. But it seems plain to me that much bigger issues are involved than the proper punishment of one man. For myself I would rather see him go free than let him incite the storm of race feeling and antagonism that will ravage our relations with these people if the case comes up again" (128). Arden feels that the courts should be the final authority, because they reflect the local and human aspect of justice: "The high-water mark of British justice is found in the Courts. If it is tempered with mercy here and expediency there, that is because it is human, or perhaps because it is divine. But for Heaven's sake let us leave it to its appointed medium. Nothing could be madder than the attempt to do it violence for its own good" (128). Arden's view is that the human tempering of the principle with local interests is justifiable in the circumstances. Yet the viceroy persists in his imposition of absolute equality; Morgan is retried and sentenced to be hanged. Arden's belief that his local judge had found a reasonable compromise with a murky situation proves correct when the evidence against Morgan proves false, although Duncan implies that Morgan's subsequent death by suicide is really no great loss.

The lesson of Set In Authority is pronounced by Victoria Tring, Lord Thame's fiancée; when questioned by her relatives as to her opinion of the case, she replies that she believes that, in such cases, it is best to trust "the man on the spot" (102). She means to trust

Thame, but the significance carries further; Thame should have trusted Arden, who, in the end, trusted his "man on the spot," the local judge Hossein. Hossein's verdict of culpable homicide and his light sentence, which satisfied everyone and avoided an inter-racial clash, are perhaps as close to justice as it is possible to get under the conditions of rural India, and only the "man on the spot" can judge.

Victoria Tring and Mrs Arden are the two women whose expertise and advice prove useful in the novel. Victoria's significant first name corresponds with her imperialist views; she refuses to marry Thame and go with him to India because she disagrees with his belief that Britain should withdraw from the colony. She states unequivocally that the experience of ruling will change his mind, and it does; when he returns, convinced of the importance of the eastern colonies and of the importance of the British "civilizing mission," they marry. Mrs Arden, who is pitied by her husband for being merely bright and not brilliant, quietly fosters her husband's friendship with the viceroy and smoothes his relations with the local officials of Ghoom with her own sociable manner. Her gift of creating bonds of love and obligation among those officials who must work together is unacknowledged by her husband until after her death.

Reconciliation of eternal principles and diverse local conditions, between the centralized government of the Empire and the necessity for local autonomy in the colonies, might be possible in theory, but the tension between the two persists in Duncan's work. Nothing less than human selfishness opposes the Empire, and such selfishness cannot be overcome by individual legislative reforms, no matter how highly motivated. Yet, like many of her contemporaries in Canada, Duncan resolves the tension by depicting the Empire as an ideal of human striving. The achievement of the unified Empire would require a kind of renewal of the human spirit, accomplished by the preservation of the "moral advantage" that the Canadians, however jealous of their political autonomy, share with the British. Like other colonials, Duncan was suspicious of the attempt to unilaterally apply eternal principles in the diverse local conditions of the Empire; the loyalty, affection, sympathy, and love implied by the marriage metaphor and the reality of marriages between characters in the novels offers a way to reconcile central principles with the places and the peoples on the margins of the Empire.

The First World War: Mending the Broken Teacup

The advent of the First World War shifted and refocused Duncan's point of view towards the war effort. While her earlier work had emphasized the differences between the three countries of the North Atlantic triangle, under the threat of a war with Germany the colonial perspective of *His Royal Happiness* (1914), *Title Clear* (1922), and *The Gold Cure* (1924) emphasized the similarities that would bring the US into alliance with Britain and Canada. The preservation of ideals of loyalty and faithfulness, first articulated by Duncan as typical of the colonial perspective, is the imperative that reunites Britain and the US in these three novels and in the many plays that Duncan wrote during the war. The feminine focus on maintaining ties between countries, which Duncan emphasized in her novels dealing with the Empire, expands to include the US for the propagandistic purpose of persuading the Americans to declare war in concert with England, rather than to quietly reap profits from trade with her former allies.

By the beginning of the twentieth century, a war between Germany and Britain had begun to seem inevitable to many British commentators and novelists. The Boy Scout movement and its emphasis on "preparedness" for an invasion of German troops was the premise of a group of popular novels, dubbed "invasion literature" and parodied by P.G. Wodehouse in *The Swoop*. Duncan had remarked upon Germany's increasing industrial rivalry with England in her review of *Made in Germany* by E.E. Williams, in which, she recounts, the author demonstrates "how during recent years the manufacturing trades of England – have been and are being outrivaled by competitors on the continent."[1] The publication of Williams's book evidently sparked a controversy in England which was reported later in the *Indian Daily News* when Lord Roseberry replied to Williams's claims, citing an article in *The Economist* that claimed that German competition was effective in only a few sectors of the economy.[2] Still, Germany's industrial might, colonial ambitions, and growing navy seemed to threaten a clash with Britain in the near future.

The question in the minds of many Britons was where the United States would stand in the event of a war between the two European powers. The US had recently proclaimed the Monroe Doctrine, which unilaterally declared that no imperialist ambitions other than its own would be tolerated on the American continents. The doctrine was seen by many as a direct challenge to Britain. When Venezuela's border dispute with British Guiana provoked the appearance of British warships, the US responded by sending its own navy to skirmish with the British, and war between the US and Britain was narrowly averted.

Duncan followed the Venezuelan dispute in the pages of the *Indian Daily News*, which ridiculed the American contention that its ships were intended to assist its weak neighbour in a just cause and warned that the US, far from simply intervening in one dispute, "hopes for the eventual withdrawal of European rule from the American continent."[3] She believed that the US was spoiling for a fight, egged on by the senate, and interpreted US designs on Cuba several months afterwards as deliberate provocation: "In its exhibition of perfectly irrational war feeling the Senate at Washington has afforded the world ... an almost unparalleled instance of the folly which often waits upon over prosperity."[4] When an Anglo-American tribunal was proposed to settle such dangerous disputes, Duncan welcomed the suggestion: "The proposed tribunal may be the beginning of that better and closer understanding among all branches of English-speaking people so rapidly expanding into nations, which will end in their federation for the ideal ends of civilization."[5] The negotiation and the consequences of such a treaty became the focus of her first "war book," *His Royal Happiness*, published in 1914.

As the First World War progressed, many of the ideological changes that historians now associate with it became evident: loss of faith in the "imperial project"; loss of belief in Britain's military might and in abstract ideals in general; and increasing acceptance of materialist goals and individualism. In response to the loss of ideal vision, Duncan's work presents her colonial perspective of idealism over material gain and alliance instead of confrontation. She began to write plays with the propagandistic purposes of encouraging enlistment and castigating conscientious objectors as hypocrites and profiteers. Using the public forum of the stage in its traditional role as platform for ideas, she addressed specific issues such as the Irish nationalists' refusal to join the British army, and government pensions for common-law wives of soldiers. Both plays and novels continue the feminine focus on preserving connections, using international marriages as allegory for, and alternative to, political alliances; they develop this motif further by showing the importance of the kind of marriage – motivated by love or by money, forced or chosen. The introduction of the possibility of "rape" by Germany (in the undated play *Teaching English*) makes women's bodies the battlefield for the defence of Victorian values.

DUNCAN'S COLONIAL PERSPECTIVE as a Canadian and a woman assured her belief in the importance of creating and maintaining ties between countries. From her earliest journalism on, she adopted the concept of an "Anglo-Saxon race," descended from the ancient tribes of Britain, to express her view that Britain, the colonies, and the United States were essentially united by their common heritage. In her view, the American War of Independence which sundered that unity was an abberation, the result of inflexibility on the British side and quickness to anger on the American. Duncan expressed her colonial point of view by arguing, with her contemporaries, that Canada was uniquely positioned to mediate between the Empire and the United States, and suggesting that Canada would be the agent whereby the US could be persuaded to rejoin the family of the Anglo-Saxon race.

As historians Joseph Levitt and Carl Berger have stated, the process of defining Canada in relation to the Anglo-Saxon race was in itself a nationalist strategy. Levitt points out: "Glorifying the Anglo-Saxon race made good nationalist sense because it increased pride in the British heritage and made it possible to envisage a greater Canadian role in world politics as a 'linchpin' connecting the British and the Americans."[6] Duncan's idealization of Canada as a middle path between the extremes of Britain and the United States allowed for an emphasis on the colonial heritage, yet it also allowed for the portrayal of Canadians as actors in international politics. Canada's unique nature made Canadians the force that could bring together the disparate elements of the Anglo-Saxon race for trade, mutual defence, and the aims of world peace.[7]

Popular use of the term "race" showed little sense of its biological meaning. Sporadic attempts to prove the discrete character of the "Anglo-Saxon race" or the "English-speaking peoples" were often based on cultural traditions such as the primitive parliaments of the Germanic peoples[8] or the supposed administrative instinct of the English. The idea of evolution was applied to culture and language in the concept, for example, of the evolution of modern languages from a common Indo-European tongue. The phrase "English-speaking race" indicates that race was bound up with the concepts of culture and nationality as well as colour of skin or configuration of skull. Certainly, many did include in their idea of Anglo-Saxonism the inherent right of the "higher" races to enslave or even exterminate the "lower," usually non-white, peoples: Theodore Roosevelt's justifications of the Indian Wars[9] and US imperial ambitions in Spanish North America in the late nineteenth century often appealed to race,[10] as did some discussions of British rule in India. However, many imperialists who, like Duncan and George Parkin, were popular idealists did not consciously include the concept of racial superiority to other peoples in their idea of race. For Parkin, as well as for Duncan, the term "Anglo-Saxon race" "defined the white people of the United Kingdom and the Dominions (and in some contexts the United States as well) who had acquired over the generations certain common racial instincts based on shared history, commercial energy, climate, parliamentary traditions, religion and culture, a group which for all important purposes were one in emotions, traditions and ideals".[11] Common characteristics ascribed to the Anglo-Saxon race were a special facility for organizing, love of liberty, and a facility for abstract reasoning that resulted in a high moral sense. Parkin states, "It is generally supposed that the Anglo-Saxon people are most strongly influenced by reason, by arguments directed to their intelligence,"[12] and Darwin had believed that the ability to use reason correctly led to a "higher" morality.[13] The evolution of British representative democracy was thought to indicate the racial characteristics of love of freedom and ability for organization. Parkin believed that "a special capacity for political organisation may, without race vanity, be fairly claimed for Anglo-Saxon people,"[14] and he called upon that power to be put to use not in subjugating other peoples but in solving the details of Imperial Federation.

The term "race" was used with little consistency among literary and political writers in Canada, and Duncan similarly is imprecise in her connection of race with any consistent biological entity. Archibald Lampman states that the United States has already formed a separate race, marked by "certain noticeable American peculiarities of mind and character." He speculates on a future Canadian race that will "combine the energy, the seriousness, the perseverance of the Scandinavians with something of the gayety [sic], the elasticity, the quickness of spirit of the south."[15] Using the (discredited) Lamarckian idea that physical conditions would induce hereditary variations, many imperialists argued that the Canadian climate would produce a biologically distinct race; others believed that the northern climate would ensure that the British race would prevail by discouraging immigration from warmer European countries.[16] Duncan's use of the term "race" suggests little sense of its biological basis. She says in A Daughter of Today that Americans have "an extra drop of nervous fluid," but in her journalism she portrays Americans, Canadians, and Britons as part of one race. When she mentions "blood" as a synonym for race, it does not designate a physical attribute but a kind of memory flowing from centuries of shared history. Hugh Finlay's desire to honour his engagement to his Scots fiancée is "somehow in the past and in the blood" (Imp., 168) and Lorne Murchison's explanation of the claustrophobia he felt in busy London is familiar to the townspeople of Elgin because they have "in the blood the memory of what Lorne had seen" (Imp., 128). When Lorne complains in his speech that the us has adulterated "her pure blood" by "welcoming all comers," he links the reference to blood with "polluting her lofty ideals" (Imp., 233); for Lorne, the mixing of races is an ideological, not a biological, problem.

Duncan presents the citizens of all countries colonized by the British as one race, held together by a sentiment of loyalty and familial affection that systems of government or even great injustice can do little to dent. Discussing opposition to William Gladstone's proposal for Home Rule for the Irish, Duncan remarks that any proposal for the fragmentation of the race is bound to meet defeat: "Regardless of political bias, defiant of the great hatred of iron-heeled Wrong which must possess them, it is curious to watch their wide rebellion against any scheme, though it be of alleviation, that necessitates the breaking of bonds and the subversion of sentiment."[17] American independence had seemed to break those bonds of sentiment rather abruptly; the Americans had attempted to form a new race, separate from both Canadians and Britons. But Duncan's early journalism repeatedly states that this effort is doomed to failure, for Canadians, Britons, and us citizens are, in many ways, identical peoples. In her article for *The Week*, "American Influence on Canadian Thought," she enumerates the similarities: "Like the Americans, we have a certain untrammelled consciousness of new conditions and their opportunities, in art as well as in society, in commerce, in government. Like them, having a brief past as a people, we concentrate the larger share of thought, energy and purpose upon our future. We have their volatile characters, as we would have had without contact with them; volatility springs in a new country as naturally as weeds. We have greatly their likings and dislikings, their ideas and opinions."[18] A Canadian buys an American book "in part because it is the cheapest, but in greater part because he is in every respect the sort of person whose existence in great numbers in the United States makes its publication profitable."[19] In a later article for the *Montreal Star*, Duncan reiterates the similarities between Canadians and us citizens: "The conditions of American life are largely our own conditions, and almost every feature to be praised or condemned in the civilization of our neighbours is duplicated, not quite so obtrusively, perhaps, but still duplicated amongst us. The absence of any specially recognizable agent in the development of our nationality is quite as conspicuous as it is in theirs, beyond our English inheritance of the power of conduct, which we share with them."[20] She concludes that the unique "power of opportunity" is common to the North American continent, and so common to both nationalities.[21] Moreover, both Canada and the us share an inevitable family connection with Britain, however much the us likes to deny it. In 1896, the *Indian Daily News* draws attention to the fact that us citizens are identical to the British race, "sprung from the loins of our own cockney and labouring classes, speaking our own language and aspiring to our own ambitions in most things that go to make life enjoyable."[22] It is the US tendency to deny its heritage, to insist on its independence and its democracy, that leads to its differences from Canada and Britain.

YET DESPITE THE ESSENTIAL UNITY of the Anglo-Saxon race in Duncan's novels, the citizens of various nations exhibit great variation, and Duncan's colonial roots led her towards appreciation and description of unique nationalities rather than a drive for uniformity. The surface manners that differentiate characters from the United States, Canada, and England in Duncan's novels provide not only pleasing variety and opportunity for humour but they also point to deeper differences in attitude among citizens of the three nations. The unique "identity" of an American, as Mamie Wick styles it, or the "point of view" of a Canadian, as Lorne Murchison and the Trents call it, presents the opportunity for both appreciation and constructive criticism. Britons, Americans, and Canadians need to recognize their common interests – yet that very aim can be served only by the diversity within a unified race, which allows for a constructive dialogue from many points of view.

Nowhere in her work does Duncan explicitly define "nation," or specifically cite attributes of nationalities, yet a reading of Mamie Wick, Graham and Mary Trent, Lord Peter Doleford, and Barbara Pavisay, as well as many minor figures in other novels, creates a clear composite picture of American, Canadian, and British nationalities. Mamie Wick, a representative American girl, is lively, straightforward, outspoken; she is also egotistical, lamentably misinformed about her heritage, and confused about the application of democratic principles. The British, represented by Alfred Hesketh, the Lippingtons, Christie Tod's mother (in *Title Clear*), Mr Mafferton, and others, are sincere in their attempt to accomplish good for their friends and the world, yet they are misled by selfishness and are too dependent on custom and tradition. Canadians, representing an ideal melding of the freedom of the Americans and the British respect for culture and traditional values, must learn the content of their Canadian heritage and its importance. The broad outlines of these stereotypes are immediately recognizable in late-Victorian and Edwardian fiction by authors such as Ralph Connor, Robert Barr, and Mrs Humphry Ward (and, in a more sophisticated way, Henry James).

Freedom from stifling conventionality and a sense of personal initiative are the main characteristics of America as Duncan embodies it in Mamie Wick, the heroine of *An American Girl in London*. Mamie's ability to see the British from a fresh perspective, to comment on their inflexibility and stuffiness and to encounter monuments and customs free from preconception constitutes an American "identity" (51) similar in freshness and centrality to William Dean Howells's Kitty Ellison in *A Chance Acquaintance*.[23] Yet Duncan did not ignore the common critique of American government and society in her assessment of American characters.[24] Mamie is self-centred and ethnocentric, and she continues to spout democratic rhetoric even after she recognizes her natural love of the monarchy. Similarly, American Evelyn Dicey of *Cousin Cinderella* is kind and sympathetic to her homesick Canadian friends, charming and free with her British acquaintances, yet she introduces herself into British society solely on the basis of her money and unashamedly makes friends in order to secure a husband who can make her a duchess. Mamie and Evelyn are something of a satire on the American Girl, on the order of Thomas Chandler Haliburton's Sam Slick; while Duncan admires her Americans for their energy and wit, she creates American characters who are self-condemning.

Duncan's criticism of the United States, as expressed in her American characters, is similar to that of other Canadians of her time. Many Canadians felt that because the US constitution centred on qualities such as personal freedom and individualism, it fostered an unstable personality and a chaotic community. Haliburton had complained in 1838 that the creation of one class, democratic and free in the US, makes the country particularly liable to extreme upheavals corresponding to changes in public opinion. Political corruption in the American government in the 1870s and 1880s, the accompanying violent labour/management confrontations, the Haymarket bombings, and the Monroe Doctrine seemed to be a direct result of the emancipation of human greed through the elevation of human freedom in the US constitution. Berger sums up the Canadian attitude: "Americans could have no social organization because they espoused an unworkable theory of society. Rejecting the binding force of convention and the legacies of the past, possessing no secure anchor in human nature, lacking a sense of social obligation and bereft of all principles except money-making, American society stood as living proof ... that men cannot adopt a constitution any more than they can adopt a father."[25]

Although Canadians share with Americans the volatility, the personal freedom, and the natural equality that seem endemic to North America, the former are saved from the excesses of American character by their preservation of the British heritage in the form of the British constitution. The Trents of *Cousin Cinderella* (1908) exemplify the way that Canadians naturally feel kinship with British ideals. Mary and Graham both yearn to be "part of" London; Graham busies himself rescuing symbols of British culture from sale to Americans. Mary's recognition of Lord Peter Doleford's relation to the ideals of the "race" plays a great part in her love for him: "Lord Doleford's features at once suggested a race and then a type and then an order, and a kind of direct correspondence of character ... it was that sign of purpose and intention, which would be, one felt, as simple and as high as modern circumstances permitted" (108). Pavis Court, the ancestral home of Doleford's family, also embodies an ideal to which the Canadians respond. Graham's engagement to Barbara is a kind of personal sacrifice to save that ideal from the auction block: "What lives and hearts and fortunes had it not already devoured, that old exquisite stone house! And all with what an air of detachment, almost of irony, before such sacrifices to its uplifted ideal, an air that said, 'What are your foolish human complications to me? I have to do with beauty, not at all with you' (241–2). But, for Duncan, the British heritage of ideals has also been practically obscured by materialism and the overwhelming weight of conventionality. Mamie Wick criticizes her British readers by remarking that "You are never in the least amused at yourselves" (AG, 190). Her friend Charlie Mafferton epitomizes the British devotion to custom: "It took very little acquaintance with Mr. Mafferton to know that, if he had never seen it done, he would never do it" (AG, 178). The British aristocrats in *Cousin Cinderella* are frankly interested in colonials only if they are rich and marriageable. Blind adherence to social rules make Britons akin to "a depository of views and archives" (229) rather than living beings, and life in Britain is a kind of incarceration (8).

Because Canada inherited British ideals, enlivened by North American freedom and initiative, Duncan locates the possibility of an ideal social order in Canada. While the British, Americans, and Indians are undeniably other – "them" – to Duncan, the Canadians are "us." The farmers of *The Imperialist* represent the "development between" Britain and America; Duncan depicts their ability to respond to ideals, in spite of their inborn selfishness, as creating the closest approximation to an ideal society. Mary Trent's Canadian upbringing has made her able to understand British ideals and to long to be part of London; yet she is enabled to feel a "divine disdain" of the city when she realizes that the Canadian birthright of freedom and independence is "something as precious in its way ... as any opportunity or any possession, something which gave even Pavis Court one aspect of a mess of pottage" (cc, 310). The Canadian ability to join both ideality and reality, monarchy and democracy, connectedness and independence makes Canadians able to mediate between the us and Britain in *His Royal Happiness*, and to see other cultures clearly in all three novels.

FROM HER EARLIEST JOURNALISM to her last few novels, Duncan speculates on the possibility of reunifying the Anglo-Saxon race by treaty with the us. Duncan sees differences between Canada, the us, and Britain only in their degree of commitment to British ideals; the different kinds of political organization that characterize all three she dismisses as matters that can easily be fixed. In her early fiction she treats as speculative the possibility of the reunification of the race within a revitalized Empire, but as the threat of the First World War becomes more real, she seriously discusses the necessity for an alliance in *His Royal Happiness* (1914).

The idea of "unification" or "reunification" of the Anglo-Saxon race arose in the late-nineteenth-century English-speaking community with a variety of implications. Italy and Germany had recently united under one central government, and Germany especially was becoming a threat to British commercial and naval superiority in Europe. The necessity for Britain to secure markets for its manufactured goods was becoming evident; independence and industrial development in the colonies had succeeded the old mercantilist policies of Empire, and some kind of commercial or military alliance seemed to be necessary to counter the common fear of Japan and Russia and the new trade empire of Germany. Joseph Chamberlain in England originally proposed an alliance with Germany; when this failed, he took up the colonial idea of Imperial Federation, which would provide a common market as well as common defence and foreign policy for Britain and the self-governing colonies. Roosevelt, his Secretary of State John Hay, and Senators Henry Cabot Lodge and Albert Beveridge worked to create an "English speaking people's league of God for the permanent peace of this war-torn world."[26] But this movement had to contend with a population that was significantly non-British in origin and generally anglophobic, and the proposals were defeated.

In *His Royal Happiness* (1914), Duncan dramatizes Canada's mission as a mediator between Britain and the United States. The protagonist is the British prince Alfred, the youngest son of the royal family. Alfred's health is delicate and is worsened by his frustration at constantly following rules of protocol. He falls in love with the American heiress Hilary Lanchester and marries her a few hours before his friend Youghall brings news of his brothers' deaths. Alfred leaves Hilary to take up his responsibilities as king; diplomatic complications prevent him from acknowledging his wife for five years.

Although Alfred is the protagonist of the novel, his Canadian friend Arthur Youghall might more properly be called the hero. Youghall realizes that Alfred embodies the aspirations of the race, and that a solution to the problem posed by his unacknowledged wife must be found that satisfies both his instincts for British tradition and his instincts for personal freedom. Youghall acts as go-between for the couple, and works through the Foreign Office to negotiate a treaty that cements a political alliance between Britain and the US and allows the marriage to seem a natural outcome.

Duncan introduces the mediating role of Canada metaphorically with a tea-party involving Alfred and his Oxford friends Youghall, Longworth (from the United States), and Manners (from Yorkshire):

He himself was pouring the tea, stretching his hand from where he sat to give the last drop of it to Longworth, from Massachusetts, who held his cup over the back of the chair he bestrode; and Prince Alfred tipped the pot at such a determined angle, that the lid dropped into the cup and knocked a three-cornered bit out.

"Now you've done it, Cakes," remarked Longworth, considering the damage.

"It'll mend all right" said Youghall, a Rhodes man, from St. John, New Brunswick, ducking for the piece. (8–9)

Longworth, whose casual manner and characteristic pose were nurtured in the home state of the Boston Tea Party, represents the American side of the War of Independence; Alfred, zealously pursuing his own ends, breaks the teacup. But the Canadian offers a solution: "It will mend," he repeats, "if you will take care of the pieces" (10).

Prince Alfred, whose nickname "Cakes" indicates his mission, has the natural characteristics to reunite the exponents of republican democracy with the subjects of the monarch. Prince Alfred has a patrician appearance, in keeping with his heredity, but the "democratic ideal" (4) (as distinct from the practice of democratic politics) is also part of him through his racial inheritance. Duncan underscores the duality of Alfred's nature by giving him a uniquely significant history at Oxford: rather than taking a "Gentleman's Third," the prince democratically insists on sitting exams in his specialty, American history, and proves his superiority by taking a First.

Alfred's health is dependent on the recognition of both elements of his character and the maintenance of a balance between the two. *His Royal Happiness* is not a story of Alfred's personal liberation from stifling tradition, nor is the point of the novel only that "the weight of English tradition cripples the soul and American freedom liberates it."[27] English tradition lives in Alfred, as Duncan demonstrates in his emotional reaction to his introduction in the US congress, where he finds "himself for the first time in his life vividly standing for his country" (47). Certainly Alfred's illness is partially caused by the lack of "the personal stimulus" (128) that his position imposes, but Alfred's treatment by an American doctor helps him to make up the "personal equation" of tradition and freedom and to allow him, like his Canadian friend, to exhibit all the virtues of his inheritance. He returns to England to regain his health and introduce his own style of monarchy, taking back the personal initiative stripped from the Crown by Parliament and proving himself an able statesman.

In an article published in *The Week* twenty-eight years before the publication of *His Royal Happiness*, Duncan had ridiculed the idea of an American queen: "To give the matter serious thought is to be scandalised and repelled by the idea to a very unpleasant degree. Commercial ties, a common faith, and the community of sentiment existing between peoples of similar institutions, are all that is necessary to bind the United States to the Mother Country."[28] By the time Duncan wrote *His Royal Happiness*, the world situation had changed and so had her opinion. The United States seemed to need a reminder of its community of sentiment with other English-speaking nations, especially as the expanding European commercial empires threatened traditional British markets. The romantic reconciliation of the two countries through the marriage of Alfred and Hilary may have some elements of fantasy, but the book is also a persuasive tract to convince the US where its sentiments should lie in the coming war. To rationalize the apparent lowering of standards that an American bride implies, Duncan makes Hilary Lanchester's ancestors British aristocrats and her godmother is Alfred's aunt, the Princess Georgina.

Alfred's position as king does not allow him to make overtures to an anglophobic United States, incited against him by yellow journalism and election fever. Alfred needs the help of his Canadian friend Youghall. Youghall is dedicated to the ideal of the reconciliation of the Anglo-Saxon race. For him, an alliance between Britain and the United States is a natural solution to the unnatural state of division: "The world is too small for new races, old man. You can't make one out of two hundred years and a few flavourings from Europe. We're one lot and, please God! nothing of so little consequence as a form of government shall permanently divide us, or our inheritance" (325). Youghall engineers the treaty of alliance, and he digs out an obscure legal point to secure Alfred's marriage to Hilary against the opposition of his family and his prime minister (315–16). Youghall responds to Alfred as both monarch and man, and so secures the ideal of unity of the race.

Significantly, the bride that Alfred's family has chosen for him is a member of the European Saxe-Cobourg family, a girl who attended school with Hilary Lanchester and who is already in love with someone else. The German desire to force her into an unnatural and loveless alliance with England is foiled by Alfred's recovery of his strength and Youghall's exacting knowledge of British law. The motif of a loveless marriage between England and Germany, perhaps enforced by violence, recurs in many of Duncan's wartime plays.

Duncan's plays[29] display many characteristics of the popular Edwardian comedy, relying on switched identities, disguised twins, slapstick stage business, and dialect for their humour. *Good Dog* and a dramatization of Duncan's popular children's novel, *The Story of Sonny Sahib* (dated 1894 by Thomas Tausky), are clearly apprentice work, relying as they do on the acting abilities of dogs, horses, and monkeys as well as children and rather large casts of adults. There is no evidence that either was ever performed. But of the remaining plays – including *Mrs Bobby Bigamist*, *Teaching English*, *Billjim from Down Under* (performed in Adelaide, Australia, according to an undated clipping from the *Adelaide Register*), *Julyann* (performed in 1917), *Beauchamp and Beecham* (produced at the Lyric Theatre in 1916), *A Knight of Two Hats*, *Title Clear* (marked "Revised Oct. 29, 1920"), and *The Gold Cure* – several were performed as benefits for war charities and received good reviews.[30] Two letters in the collection indicate that Everard Cotes was unsuccessful in promoting at least two of them after Duncan's death.

All of the plays are comedies, primarily concerned with creating suitable marriages for the protagonists. "Suitable" marriages are no longer as obvious as they used to be, for class lines have blurred as old families lose their fortunes in the war and noblemen refuse commissions in order to fight among the enlisted men. Among the "ideal" virtues that identify the male heroes of the plays, the most important is willingness to enlist; after that, a modest income (however derived), good manners, education, and a belief in the ideals and future of England are common to heroes. International marriages are usually between Americans and Britons, although in *Billjim from Down Under* Australia comes to Britain's rescue as the title character marries his British sweetheart.

In all the plays, making money and marrying for money are explicitly contrasted with the idealism of supporting the war effort. In *Julyann*,[31] a comedy set mainly in Ireland, Jim Gallagher accuses the Irish nationalists who refuse to enlist of using politics as an excuse to stay home and profiteer (act 3, 30). Lizzie Lacey, a minor character who returns from America to become a war nurse, states that the us has stayed out of the war because "ivery one in America was runnin' as if a dog was afther them chasin' the dollars" (act 2, 33); she refuses a substantial raise in her job as a department store clerk and quits to become a nurse. "Says I to the boss, 'You can stay here an' make the money. I'm goin' where they're makin' the war,' I says" (act 2, 9). In *The Gold Cure*, the Hon. Roddy Trenchard's family wants him to marry the heiress, Bella Box, rather than the heroine, Betty Van Allen; while Bella is identified as a "millionaire's daughter" in the novel version, the play specifically calls her father a war "profiteer" (act 1, 23). Betty herself is courted by Lansing Carter, whose materialism is signalled by his avowal of his love (also unique to the dramatic version): "There's nothing on God's earth I won't get her, if she wants it" (act 1, 7). In *Mrs. Bobby Bigamist*, the heroine Joyce Allen is forced to marry Cornelius Coker in order to support herself and her child; Coker, who is later unmasked as a German spy, is making a fortune trading in rationed foodstuffs while his rival for Joyce's love, a poor soldier, risks his life.

As in Duncan's earlier novels, marriage becomes an important signal of British international alliances and a tangible alternative to more abstract diplomatic ties. In *Mrs. Bobby Bigamist*, the identity of Joyce Allen's sinister German husband is discovered before the marriage is consummated, and Joyce remarries her "Tommy" sweetheart. In *Billjim from Down Under*, an Australian soldier offers to marry the widowed common-law wife of a British officer, thus symbolically representing the colonial who willingly takes on the responsibilities of the wounded motherland. In *Title Clear, The Gold Cure, A Knight of Two Hats, Teaching English*, and *Julyann*, a marriage between British and American protagonists seals the alliance of the two countries in wartime.

The possibility of a British "marriage" with Germany and the nature of such a marriage is explored in *Mrs. Bobby Bigamist* and *Teaching English*. In both, the Germans use physical force and financial blackmail in an attempt to force sexual relations on English women, in a parallel to the violence taking place in Europe. In *Mrs. Bobby Bigamist*, Cornelius Coker buys up all of Joyce Allen's debts and presses her for payment, forcing her to marry him in order to support herself. She refuses sexual relations with him until the end of the war as a memorial to her fallen soldier husband, and his constant badgering on his rights as a husband threaten to take a violent turn. In *Teaching English*, the German count Von Furstig uses a whip and military discipline to force the Englishwoman Hilda Creyke to forsake her American fiancé and become his mistress. His actions are linked to a philosophical system of relativistic morals and utility: "Gott – why yes we haf Gott. Und devil also we haf devil – Ha ha! We drive them together in the service of the State. Neither vice nor virtue Miss Hilda, but only utility in the service of the State" (act 3, 30). In the final scene of this unashamedly melodramatic piece, the count's female compatriots declare, "We have not philosophised ourselves out of civilization," and help the young Englishwoman escape with her American airman.

As this brief account reveals, the artistic aim of these plays is not very high. Their lack of subtlety may simply be the result of the translation of Duncan's ideas to the less subtle form of the stage; Edwardian drama (and late-Victorian drama, for that matter) was not, in the main, noted for being understated. The purpose of the plays seems to have been unabashedly patriotic, and they may have represented the same kind of "war work" for the author that they advocate for the female characters; the patriotism of the early twentieth century, relying as it does on militarism and racial stereotype, is offensive to the post-modern reader. While many of the plays were performed several times in major theatres and may have enjoyed substantial runs "in the country," Duncan was not very successful as a dramatist, and these plays demonstrate why.

The women in Duncan's plays are important to the war effort, not only as industrial workers and nurses but also as builders of the international alliances that will help to win the war for Britain. Yet the plays themselves show an ambivalent attitude towards the new feminism sparked by women's work during the war years. In *Mrs. Bobby Bigamist*, three women approach Joyce Allen to use her influence with her husband in the service of "causes": Miss Allen fights for women's right to continue to work after the war, Mrs Tump fights for temperance, and Miss Skillington focuses on "uplifting the German people after the war." Joyce Allen objects to the lowering of vision and the loss of faith implied by all three causes: "Did nature commit a crime when she made a butterfly? Such happy little butterflies we were, a little while ago – friends of the flowers, loving the sun! And now such a lot of us – poor little grubs again – grubby little black grubs – and the flowers and the sunshine are for somebody else" (act 2, 10).

But Duncan herself crusades for a feminist cause in *Billjim from Down Under*. The plot concerns a young woman who has given birth to an illegitimate child; her soldier lover died before they could be married and so she is not entitled to a widow's pension or a government allowance to support her baby. The mother laments, "I have no child – that the State can or will acknowledge.

No name, no place, no help, no allowance, for me or my baby" (act 2, 43). Ruby Laughton, the heroine, writes a letter to solicit donations to help such children: "If the men and women of England are going to protect tomorrow the ideals they are fighting for today, every child born to those ideals must be given the best possible start in life" (act 3, 29).

DUNCAN'S LAST TWO NOVELS, *Title Clear* and *The Gold Cure*, are clearly commercial love stories, with little of the dramatic intensity characteristic of the political novels of her early and middle career. Both contain dialogue almost identical to the dramatized versions of the same stories. Yet both are interesting for their depiction of the central colonial theme of reunifying the race by bringing the United States back into the Empire. In both novels, the reunification is carried out without the agency of Canada; the imminence of the First World War seemed to demand direct action. *Title Clear* (published in 1922) is the story of Campbell Fraser, a young man forced by British inflexibility to leave his native Scotland and emigrate to the United States. Fraser returns incognito twenty-three years later, a self-made millionaire, to discover that the town of Kirkiebrig remains the same and that his sweetheart, Christina Tod, has expressed "the ideal of faithfulness" to his memory even though he was reported killed in the Boer War. Fraser finds that he still loves Christina and Kirkiebrig, but before he can possess them he must acknowledge his desertion from the Boer War and his parallel desertion of Christina, a desertion from duty and family which parallels the American War of Independence. Both he and his American-born son eventually die in France, their deaths symbolizing the sacrifice that brings the two cultures together in defence of the values they hold in common. Christina's memorial to her lover, a stone cross set at the crossroads of the town, fills the "empty heart" (13) of Kirkiebrig: "The cross seems to stand on the very heart of Kirkie now, and never lacks a wreath" (288).

Duncan's last novel, *The Gold Cure* (1924), clearly expresses some of the most central social and political ideas of her career. The "gold cure" of the title is the cure for gold hunger; transcendent ideals triumph over materialistic considerations in the marriage of the American heroine, Betty Van Allen, to the British lord Roddy Trenchard. The novel begins as Betty rejects a marriage in which she would have been little more than a decorative prop to her husband's shady business career; she flees to England disguised as her Irish maid. Alone and broke in London, Betty finds use for her typing skill, which she acquired in order to be financially independent. She meets Roddy, son of an ancient but impoverished noble family; concealing her identity as an American heiress to the last, she ensures that her marriage is based on the "magic" of chivalry and self-sacrifice rather than anticipation of her father's money. Instead of marriage to a stockbroker, who symbolizes the profiteering of the non-productive rich, she chooses independence and, finally, a marriage with her new English fiancé, cementing the family tie between North America and Britain and bringing new money into an old, aristocratic family. Roddy is saved from his engagement to the lower-class daughter of a war profiteer who is obsessed by the material in the form of business dealings and conspicuous consumption.

Twenty years earlier, Duncan had asserted the essential unity of the British, American, and Canadian peoples in *A Daughter of Today* (1894). Janet Cardiff tells her American friend, "We're a conventional people ... And so are you, for how could you change your spots in a hundred years?" (115). Although the tone of Duncan's work during and after the war is considerably more sentimental than that of *A Daughter of Today*, the idea expressed is a common one: the unity of the Anglo-Saxon race in its commitment to ideals beyond the material, and the expression of that unity in common support for Britain.

CHAPTER EIGHT

Race: "On the Other Side of a Prejudice"

Sara Jeannette Duncan could not escape the racism inherent in the characterization of the British as a distinct race; as Edward Said points out, the late-nineteenth-century "habit of deploying large generalisations by which reality is divided into various collectives: languages, races, types, colours, mentalities,"[1] is not so much a recognition of neutral difference between groups "as an evaluative interpretation" of their position in a hierarchy. In his book *Orientalism*, Said argues that the European discourse of imperialism, in India as elsewhere, assumed the existence of a discrete and monolithic category, "the Oriental," which was primitive, unchanging, homogeneous. The "Oriental Mind," created as irretrievably other than the rational "Occident," was characterized by its "sensuality, its tendency to despotism, its aberrant mentality, its habits of inaccuracy, its backwardness."[2] Above all, the Orient was created as open to generalized description and characterization by the Occident, a dynamic in which the West assumed the position of authority over the passive East. Such ideas were not confined to a few racists; Orientalism as institutionalized in academic and political theory was latent in much of the "scientific" research of nineteenth-century Europe and provided a general theory for imperial military and political administration.

Duncan's writings about India assume the hierarchy that Said finds latent in the discourse of nineteenth-century imperialism. For Duncan, the supposed Anglo-Saxon special facility for political administration makes the British the rulers of India, and the Indian habituation to despotic government makes them subordinate. Significantly, she does not ascribe these positions to biology, but to cultural inheritance; the British have inherited political ideals that lead them to use power for compassionate rather than selfish ends and to use political freedom in a responsible way, while the Indians must acquire such ideals through education and observance of the British example. The races of India are therefore not destined to die out, or to give way before the British, but to meld what is good about their own cultures with the political ideals of England. However, it matters little whether the differences between the rulers and the ruled are genetic or cultural; in Duncan's novels Indians are not fit to govern themselves, and only in some individual cases are they fit to associate on a basis of friendly equality with Britons.

But despite this acceptance of the basic hierarchy which justifies Britain's imperial project, Duncan expresses her colonial perspective by trying to write against the centre, showing both her acceptance and her suspicion of totalizing generalizations about race. As a woman and a colonial, Duncan had been a victim of such generalizations: her Canadian characters must patiently explain to the British that Canada is not always frozen, that Canadians do not always want to come "Home" to retire; her female characters must vehemently deny that self-sacrifice comes naturally to women and that all women are naturally motherly. All the characteristics that Said finds applied to the Orient in nineteenth-century imperialist texts – cruelty, passivity, inability to tell the truth, lack of "moral development" – have at various times up to the present been used to characterize women as well. Thus the Oriental is feminine, and Duncan follows her practice of asserting the importance of the feminine qualities of sentiment and connection in showing the importance of the preservation of the Indian spiritual inheritance and the importance of sympathy and affection to creating a bond between Indian and Briton. Thus, when she comes to characterize individual Indians, she creates characters who are open to British influence yet feel themselves as aliens in Anglo-Indian culture, who are confused about how much of their own culture to preserve in the balance of British ideals and Indian religion, and who yearn for the affectionate union with Britain which Duncan characterizes as a marriage. Most important, she reiterates the need to go beyond stereotypes to discover the correspondence of the ideal with the real; as she says in an article on mixed-race Eurasians in Calcutta, "On the other side of a prejudice, well-founded and well built, who knows what fruits may drop and what flowers grow. Nothing is more certain than that we can not see over it."[3]

THE CONCEPT OF BIOLOGICAL RACE predated Charles Darwin, but it became a topic of current discussion after the publication of *The Descent of Man* (1871) and the works of Herbert Spencer. Darwin argued that all men were descended from "a hairy, tailed quadruped, probably arboreal in its habits";[4] while he believed that all races of man belonged to a common biological species, he stressed the importance of evolution of the "moral faculties" through the use of reason and used this criterion to determine advanced and backward races. Moreover, he stated that "backward races would disappear before the advance of higher civilizations."[5] As a result of the widespread discussion of Darwin's evidence and his conclusion, the biological model of competitive species was commonly applied to many aspects of human life, often with little accuracy.[6]

Comments published in the *Indian Daily News* on the Jameson Raid of 1896 (a prelude to the Boer War of 1898–1902) indicate acceptance of the general tenet that the "races" of the world are in violent competition for empires. An editorial in defence of Cecil Rhodes's actions on the African continent argues: "Much goes to the making of Empire which should not be too closely scrutinized ... It is with nations as it is with great families, their foundations are laid by methods which do not invariably reward examination; and it is left for those who enter into the leisure and dignity and comfort of the inheritance to indulge in regrets as to the conduct of the pioneers, and scruples as to their own."[7] In an article entitled "The Main Issue in South Africa," Duncan argues that as the Boers and the English are both European groups, both surrounded by hostile blacks, they should work together. However, she writes, it is as yet unclear whether Europeans are physically suited to life in Africa: it is "in fact by no means yet settled which is the fittest to inherit the land by survival, the European, or the Zulu, or Kaffir."[8] The *Indian Daily News*, under the editorship of Everard Cotes, generally supported Rhodes and his project of uniting southern Africa under the British crown; in Cotes's and Duncan's defence, however, it must be noted that many of the details of Rhodes's involvement in the provocation of the Boer War did not become public until many years after these comments were written.

The imperialist discourse of the late nineteenth century held that Orientals, whether Arabs, Indians, or northern Africans, were "remnants" of great races who had remained primitive or who had actually moved backward on Darwin's scale of moral evolution. Thus Oriental societies were often described as sluggish, "backward," in a state of decay or stasis. Some argued that Oriental stasis meant that England was entitled to help the Orientals along their inevitable path of extinction; but Edmund Burke's doctrine that force was to be wielded in colonies only for the tangible benefit of the inhabitants meant that social and military intervention was generally justified as an attempt to stimulate movement, or "progress," along the evolutionary scale. Such theories created the justification for social and military intervention by Europeans in India, Egypt, Palestine, and southern Africa, as well as in French, Dutch, and German colonies.

Duncan was suspicious of the new sciences that claimed to prove the superiority or inferiority of races, because they tended also to find physical explanations for the spiritual ideals she valued. She associated the biological concepts of race elucidated by Darwin and Spencer with the trend towards materialism and social science that threatened the pursuit of ideals.[9] In her novels, Spencer's belief in "higher" and "lower" races, his belief in the evolution of the moral sense through material stages rather than by gift of God, and his disbelief in God are ranged against traditional British and Hindu religious conceptions of the soul. When Sir Kristodas, in The Burnt Offering, leaves the ideals of his religion and tries to imitate the ways of the British, his change of heart is associated with a bust of Spencer on his library shelf. Joan Mills's misguided enchantment with the "Brahmo family" of Ananda Roy is a reaction against the empty spiritual life that she has endured in England; Joan tells her Indian fiancé, "I shall find it very easy to adopt your religion ... I have never been able to agree with father and Herbert Spencer" (272). The British loss of faith in their heritage is also prominently associated with science in Duncan's other novels of Indian life: Spencer's bust also looks down "with blind eyes" from a mantelpiece in Set In Authority, and the violent tendencies of Bepin Behari Dey in The Burnt Offering are associated with his degree in the natural sciences. Only a denial of materialistic science, and a joining of the ideals of both races – political and administrative on the British side, spiritual and religious on the Indian side – can resolve the differences between England and "the bride of the race."

Yet Duncan was interested in the efforts of historians and sociologists to describe and logically account for elements of the Oriental mind in an attempt to improve feeling between the British and the Indians. In an 1897 editorial, she gives an account of a lecture by "Mr. Lee-Warner" on the history of slavery in India, using his data to illuminate various aspects of Indian character, especially "indifference to death and suffering in others, and the contempt for women."[10] *Indian Daily News* editorials argue the importance of using information about local beliefs to help educate the population about cholera and other illnesses affected by sanitation. The lack of such knowledge has created, the editorials argue, a general suspicion that the British intend to secretly cause Indians to break religious taboos or to lose caste. Such suspicions were a major impediment, in Duncan's view, to the grafting of British "civilization onto an Eastern stock."[11] A later article in the *Indian Daily News* warns that "the natives, Hindu and Mahomedan, ... hate and despise them [the British] – to the knowledge of every Anglo-Indian – now. That hatred ... will continue to exist as long as native races of various religions remain, as they must remain, subject to the rule of a race which, howsoever beneficent its dominion may be, is distinctly and immutably foreign in that very matter of religion which, to the natives of India, is the main thing in life."[12] She argues that sensitive research into social customs will go some way towards alleviating that hatred.

However, Duncan showed little hope for effecting rapid social change in Indian society, and criticized the central imperialist view (often promulgated by protestant mission societies) that legislation to prevent suttee, child marriage, gambling, and similar "moral" abuses was an immediate necessity. While she does not think that Indian society is completely unchanging, she does call India "the oldest and most conservative society in the world" and recognizes that the self-righteous attempts of christian reformers to legislate away religious and social customs merely creates ill will between the two groups. In a series of editorials in the *Indian Daily News*, she deplores a scheme to outlaw the practice of gambling on the rainfall, a pastime which certain members of the Bengal council (not all Europeans, incidentally) found immoral: "These habits have not called for intervention for seventy years, and we do not believe call for any particular sudden intervention at the present moment, unless the Bengal council is about to embark on a legislation for the amelioration of the moral nature of mankind in general." Such "quite unnecessary pieces of legislation and interferences with the usages of the population of India" merely served to increase Indian suspicion of English motives.[13] An account of a speech given by Monomohum Ghose on "Anti-English Feeling in Bengal" suggests that a general lack of sympathy and knowledge displayed by the British is the source of Indian anger and hatred. The editorialist (possibly Duncan) agrees that "a great deal of harm is undoubtedly done by the attitude of those Europeans who fail to acquaint themselves with the circumstances under which the people around them live," but even more harm is done by the antagonism aroused by legislation to stop such practices as child marriage.[14]

Duncan accepts a characterization of the Oriental mind that sees it as being as unfamiliar with Western moral absolutes, whether of compassion for others or of logic and truthfulness, as it is with Western standards of cleanliness. The contrast between the two cultures is central to the plot of *Set In Authority*, in which the courts are used by an Indian victim of the 1857 Mutiny to gain revenge on a specific British regiment. The novel opens with a description of the two versions of the capital city, Pilaghur,[15] one of which "has a parade ground as well as a cathedral, and a station club where are tennis courts and the English illustrated papers, and public gardens set with palms and poinsettias, where the band plays twice a week in the evenings after polo"(21). In this Pilaghur, the sahibs quarrel over such trifles as military precedence and trespassing milch-goats, but selflessly join together in the common task of ruling India for its own good. But in "the other Pilaghur," a teeming city of beggars, water carriers, cholera, oxen, and donkeys, "there is an all-pervasive Oriental clamour and an all-pervasive Oriental smell" (24). The description of Pilaghur as Oriental would be enough to suggest to the reader an entire heritage of ideas related to the monolithic racial stereotype of dirt, drugs, lechery, poverty, overpopulation. The only individual in this Pilaghur is the grain dealer, Ganeshi Lal, who hoards food to sell to the government while his countrymen starve (24).

Yet there are positive aspects to the Oriental mind in Duncan's work, and some Indians are able to comprehend the lesson of British rule and to rise to the heights of their own culture by blending it with British ideals. Sir Ahmet Hossein, the Indian judge in *Set In Authority*, sufficiently understands ideas of British justice to reach a verdict that satisfies all concerned parties in the controversial court case that is the centre of the plot. Yet he also manages to blend his inherited religion with ideas drawn from the Jains and from Christianity, rising above the petty infighting Duncan ascribes to Indian religious zealots: "I take my religion where I can get it – a little here, a little there. This twentieth century permits that. Religion is a world product; and the time is past, I think, to fight for only one kind" (110). He captivates his friends Eliot Arden and Ruth Pearce with his account of reincarnation, and offers an alternative to the cold abstractions with which both Arden and Pearce view life.

Hossein accounts for the hostility between the British and the Indians by the lack of the sympathy, goodwill, and affection necessary for a happy union between the British governors and the "bride of the race." When Arden offers to hold a ball to introduce him to the members of the local club, Hossein exclaims with tears in his eyes, "Oh, why are there not more natures like yours among our rulers? Then would all bad feelings between the races disappear" (112). In general, Hossein is isolated and uncomfortable with the alien customs he is forced to adopt when he becomes part of the justice system: "These among whom he had come were not his people; his ways were not their ways, nor his thoughts their thoughts. Yet he had to take his place and find his comfort among them. The drift and change in the tide of events had brought him there, and he had to make the best appeal he could. In every eye he saw the barrier of race, forbidding natural motions. He would commend himself but could not do it from the heart; he was forced to take the task upon the high and sterile ground of pure intelligence" (74). Even when he expresses his emotions to Arden, the difference in customs is a barrier to full understanding. Hossein's emotionalism threatens to embarrass Arden; and when Hossein quotes William Blake's "The Little Black Boy" as an example of "the most wonderful of our poets" (112), Arden cannot repress a smile of amusement at the pronoun "our" (112).

In Duncan's books, the differences between the Indian and the British treatment of women are a major barrier to cultural equality, and an area where she agrees that the Indian is inferior. Hossein is unable to think of women as individuals, only as categories. When he meets Ruth Pearce, he responds according to his cultural limitations: "This one was of another race, and therefore remote, but she fell at the first glance into his instinctive category of the zenana. Then, as she spoke, he became aware of secondary qualities, which one must consider apart. 'Pundita,' he reflected ... and lent himself willingly to the satisfactions which a pundita could give" (77). To the Anglo-Indians of Pilaghur, Hossein's attitude to women is all-important in their decision to "know him" socially: "Mrs Lemon laid down the law"; if Hossein kept his own wife in purdah, then he would naturally consider British women immoral, and so could not be invited to dine. Happily, Mrs Lemon discovers that Hossein is married, but that his wife "preferred to live in her own native state, lacking courage to take with her husband his alarming strides of progress" (73). The question of whether his "progress" in adopting British ideals has been extended to the emancipation of women is thus deferred, and Hossein is welcomed to the club.

The central question for Indian characters in Duncan's novels is how to integrate British ideals and Indian civilization; what to adopt from Western education and what to preserve from their own heritage, and how to make the two work together in principle and reality. Their British education, dominated – in Duncan's scheme – by the new democratic politics, by sceptical modernism, and by Spencer's social science, together with an Indian heritage of Oriental poverty, mendacity, and despotism, leads the new Indian nationality towards violence and independence from Britain. But the focus of an Indian rapprochement with the British is the humane culture of British literature and Indian philosophy, which alike cultivate tolerance, religious feeling, and humility.[16]

Histories of India support Duncan's conception of Indian nationality as an amalgam of British and Indian influences. Many historians (and some novelists) judge nationalist feeling in India to be in itself foreign, created by the British themselves. In this version of history, India did not exist before foreign intervention; instead, Indians lived in a group of principalities descended from the Mughal Empire, constantly at war, with no central sense of nation to unite them. The Indian nation itself was thus formed by the British through the agency of "John Company" and, later, the Indian Civil Service when they began to unite the territories under their control (and to squeeze out uncooperative princes) in order to facilitate administration.[17] Indian nationality, and to some extent the Indian personality, is thus an amalgam of British and Indian concepts.

Difficulty in integrating the West and the East is at the heart of the political agitation against British rule in *The Burnt Offering*. The novel portrays the rise of the nationalist movement as partly the result of injudicious education: a people that has no cultural reinforcement for political order has difficulty expressing political freedom. Sir Kristodas himself expresses the view, popular in many period novels,[18] that education has hurt rather than helped India. "Macaulay inoculated us with higher education before we had the Board School. He tried to finish what had not been begun. Macaulay and Bentinck gave the Bengalis cheap intellectual stimulant, and my countrymen take to intellectual stimulant as others do to drink" (50–1). The premature introduction of university education and the years of attempting to educate Indians politically have made the nature of the government that would succeed British rule in India unpredictable, according to Ganendra Thakore. Indians now wish to be like the British, though they have no cultural tradition that would support democratic government: "'the Western model,' Ganendra smiled again. 'It is foreign to the genius of the country, and we are not like the Japanese; we do not imitate well. However,' he checked himself, 'the Western model is with us now, and we must follow. We ourselves would be content with nothing else'" (29).

The introduction of Western education and political ideas has resulted in the figure of the "Westernized Indian," represented in *The Burnt Offering* by Sir Kristodas and his daughter Rani Janaki. These two characters begin as very conventional religious Hindus: Kristodas is a representative of an ancient Brahmin family, and his daughter, married at age seven, a secluded child-widow. Before his contact with Western society, Kristodas is a compendium of virtues that would be admirable in a character from British or Indian culture: "He came of a line of pundits and poets, with more than one collateral saint, a family constantly noted for religious achievement. A flatterer told him, when he arrived at the Bench of the High Court, that he united in his person the honours of the Government and of Heaven. This was probably as true as such a sweeping compliment could be. He was famous for charity, gentleness, and austerity; no beggar was ever turned from his door, and no rule of his priestly order was ever broken within his gates" (36).

However, he "could not escape the spirit of the age" (37), and, like the socialist MP Vulcan Mills and his daughter Joan, he puts the traditional beliefs of his culture behind him. Yet Kristodas is hardly the figure of fun, or of social chaos, that the westernized Indian represents in the works of popular authors such as Edmund Candler. He is somewhat ignorant of the depth of English self-doubt (42); like Mills, he embraces modern scepticism a little too quickly, and looks with longing at the religious artifacts he relegated so summarily to the top shelf in his library. Yet he is one of the few people Mrs Foley categorizes as "just human beings" (19), and when he arrives at her party he is more a part of the social circle, "less alien to the occasion" (45) despite his Indian dress, than Mills or his daughter.

Swami Yadava, spiritual advisor to Kristodas and his family and a formidable political figure in himself, offers two metaphors for the relationship of the English and Indians. The first is the marriage, symbolized by John Game and Janaki, in which the English supply "justice, railways, political ideas ... efficiency and economy" (163) while India asks for "affection" from her rulers. While this characterization of the imperial-colonial relation does imply a difference in power as well as in function, Yadava's second metaphor places India above England. Yadava says England is a nation of men belonging by nature to the caste of *Kshattriyas*, the soldiers and rulers of Hindu India, men of action. In this scheme, India herself is equivalent to the Brahmins, devoted to contemplation, religious observance, and wisdom, yet socially above the *Kshattriyas* in a traditional hierarchy that values the things of the spirit (165–6): "What are the English but a caste, permitted by God to be the right hand of the Brahmins?" Yadava asks (166). Kristodas and Janaki accept both ideas as a natural portrayal of a working relationship that might yet exist between the two countries.

The poignancy of westernized India is expressed in the character of Janaki. To John Game, in his final days, Janaki is the embodiment of the new India, waiting for a new partnership of independence and love from England: "She stood to him for India as he thought of her – the India of his old dreams, the bride of his country, the enchantress of his race" (303). Janaki's love and sacrifice for Game are never acknowledged; instead, she is treated with unconscious condescension by Anglo-Indian ladies and receives only a bare, intellectual friendship from Game. Under the pressure of Game's preference for Joan Mills, the incarnation of modern scepticism, Janaki retreats into her Hindu widowhood. Just as Kristodas finally rejects Western science and philosophy for his traditional duties as *sanyasi*, Janaki also rejects the promise of a "marriage" with the West when she experiences the spiritual poverty of Game's rejection. Yet Janaki and Kristodas do not offer the final word on the relation between the two countries; the election in England, strongly influenced by the attempt on the life of the viceroy at the end of the novel, reconfirms the determination of Britons to maintain a relationship with India: "Sri Yadava, priest and politician, must have seen with rejoicing a husband not yet so cold" (318).

While the two revolutionaries in the novel, Bepin Behari Dey and Ganendra Thakore, are associated with violence and so are self-condemning, the emotional basis of the nationalist movement in *The Burnt Offering* is legitimate. Thakore, the nationalist leader, is identified in his courtroom scene as the soul of India, betrayed by the indecision and materialism of Victorian British rule. His final courtroom speech conveys the justification for his agitation against British rule. Thakore bases his nationalism upon a revival of Indian traditions; he calls upon a "new emotion which is beginning to thrill the hearts of my countrymen ... and through it they are finding a kind of life for their souls." Although he concedes that "it may be a feverish life. I do not ask you to believe that it is yet very sane or well regulated" (245), yet that life, the life of the soul, has a legitimacy that the novel recognizes. Thakore scorns the materialism of the West, brought to India by the British, and calls for a return to the union of God and man that his religion symbolizes: "Let others invent their luxuries, build their ships, forge their great instruments of war. The mission of India is to proclaim and to prove the union of God and man, the supreme, universal, and eternal necessity of knowledge. India holds the torch of the spirit, and would hold it high. This is the mission of Nationalism, miscalled hatred and disaffection, for the sake of which I am accused before you today" (247–8). Yadava shows a peaceful way to use the traditions of India with the ideals of the British; both nations must transcend materialism, so that the British can again become fit administrators of justice in India, and India can join in a marriage of ideals with England. Otherwise, the spectre of Bepin Behari Dey and his bombs looms large.

The problem of inter-racial marriage is not only symbolic in *The*

Burnt Offering; Janaki hopes for a marriage with John Game, and Joan Mills becomes engaged to Bepin Behari Dey. Like the international "marriages" between Britain and Canada and between Britain and the US in Duncan's other novels, the two inter-racial love stories focus on the extent to which mutual love that recognizes the importance of both partners is the motive force for the alliance. But in *The Burnt Offering,* the differing cultural conceptions of the place of women within marriage are also important. Joan's affair with the terrorist Dey is simply part of her desire to sacrifice herself for Indian culture; she is unaware that Dey already has one wife, and that the laws regarding Hindu marriage (which are protected by the British legal system in India) would allow Dey to order every detail of her life and to forbid divorce to her while allowing him to leave her "on the slightest pretext" (233). The novel implies that in marrying Dey Joan would submit to a ceremony that contradicts her ideals of freedom and denigrates her abilities as an actor in the political movement simply in order to fulfill her idea of a political sacrifice. Even Game, who loves Joan, objects to her marriage to Dey mainly because of Dey's personal character: "If she wanted to marry an Indian ... she might at least have chosen a decent fellow. There are plenty of them" (275). Janaki's love for Game, however, is based on their ability to unite the best of both cultures through love and compatibility. Janaki would be marrying for love into a society that appreciates her Indian education and relieves her of the restrictive Hindu rules for child widows. Other characters in the novel, including the very conventional Mr and Mrs Foley, encourage Janaki's relationship with Game, despite its inter-racial nature.

The marriage metaphor, which symbolizes the two cultures joined in a familial relationship (as it does in *The Imperialist,*) is centrally related to the sacrifice of the title. Mills's sacrifice of his daughter Joan in a marriage to Dey is explicitly linked to the biblical story of Abraham and Isaac (201). But the metaphor has further significance, drawn from Hindu culture. Janaki is kept from a productive alliance with Game by her religious abhorrence of a second marriage. Widowed as a young child, she continues to sacrifice to the spirit of her dead husband. Like Janaki, India is kept from a productive new union with England by her inability to adapt her religious principles to a new situation. "There are those," Yadava warns, "who would make their mother a widow"

(165). Duncan modifies the popular Victorian marriage metaphor using the topical issue of suttee – in a sense, she sees India as a widow willing to throw herself into the flames of social chaos after the death of her early marriage – rejecting the new for a celebration of death.

Duncan portrays the gap between Indian and Anglo-Saxon as very difficult to bridge; in *The Burnt Offering*, the races are "two tides that did not mingle" (120). Janaki and Game have a current of sympathy built upon their common interest in India and on Janaki's acceptance of British custom. Yet Game cannot see the cause of Janaki's unhappiness when he begins to court Joan, partly because of the cultural difference bound up in "race": "A woman of his own race would have worn her suffering differently; and he would have suspected her of exhaustion or neuralgia" (143). Game misunderstands Janaki's revelations about Thakore, wrung from her with such difficulty, as simply gossip (149–50).

Paradoxically, the two characters in *The Burnt Offering* who profess to think nothing of biological race are the most preoccupied by its effects. Joan and her socialist father, Vulcan Mills, consider many social and political questions in the novel solely in terms of their determination not to be racist, and so unconsciously focus on the racial aspect of every issue. Janaki loves Game with the blessing of her surrounding Anglo-Indian female friends, simply because she is personally attracted to him; Joan Mills, in contrast, wishes to marry Bepin Behari Dey as a statement about race relations, and feels little of Janaki's passion. When discussing "public opinion" with Lucy Foley, Joan makes a distinction between the opinion represented by Bengalis and by Europeans in Calcutta, while Lucy refers solely to "the people who have made the place, and keep it" (118). Mrs Maybird's "Ladies' League" party confirms that opinion is as diverse among Bengalis as it is between Joan and Lucy, yet Joan tries to make Bengalis into a monolithic group.

Duncan, of course, had another model of two cultures living together, drawn from her Canadian experience. A number of editorials on the Manitoba Schools Question in 1896 form a commentary on the British project of amalgamating British and Indian cultures. Duncan argues that protecting French customs by legislation has effectively prevented the peaceful co-existence of French and English in Canada: "With curious lack of foresight,

and an excessive consideration probably arising from the experienced effect of harshness in dealing with other [conquered peoples]
the Home Government gave the conquered French provinces of
Canada, by the British North America Act, various unnecessary
privileges ... Thus all possibility of the amalgamation of the French
with the British Canadian was forever destroyed."[19] Duncan's opinions on French Canadians can be extended to India and Britain;
clearly she suggests that the protection of Indian culture from
contact with British is not the way to assure peace between the
two cultural groups. Rather, the adoption of British ideals and
British customs is portrayed as an advantage to Indians, along with
the preservation of their own culture's religious ideals as an antidote
to modern scepticism and materialism.

   An unstated hierarchy is the focus of Duncan's portrayal of British
and Indians in her Indian novels. Duncan depicts Indians as separate and different from Anglo-Indians; she rationalizes the British
presence in India by agreeing that the Indian heritage, though rich
in insights into human character and the emotional and religious
life, does not provide the virtues of organization, temperance, and
tolerance that lead to good self-government. Yet, unlike the majority of Anglo-Indian novelists and writers on Empire, she finds
good and useful aspects of Indian culture; she portrays Indians as
motivated by their personal lives and their culture towards peace
and good fellowship among themselves and with Anglo-Indians.
Such awareness of difference might easily be termed racism by the
modern critic. But Duncan also focuses on Americans and Britons
as different; she creates "typical examples" of Americans, Britons,
and Indians. Her strategy of "othering"[20] Britons or Americans by
identifying a corporate "they" who share physical and psychological characteristics is common to her portrayal of all nationalities
except her own, and focuses on defining rather than penalizing
the excluded group.

   Such strategies might also be seen in the light of theories of
creating fictional "types" or typical examples of a kind of person
who appears in real life; Janet Cardiff defends such techniques in
A Daughter of Today (115). The "typical" American girl, British lord,
or Canadian hero are stock figures in late Victorian and Edwardian
popular novels.[21] Duncan's creation of "typical" Indians, such as
the "Bengali gentlemen" journalists of His Honor, and a Lady, or the
British-loving Ahmet Hossein of Set In Authority, must be viewed

in the literary context of a theory of national types as well as of an overwhelmingly racist surrounding society.

Duncan's strategy of writing against the racist stereotype of the Indian might be distinguished by the concept of "closure." The racist sees "the other" as a closed object, monolithic and unchanging, defined solely by difference from the subject. Duncan avoids closure by presenting Indian opinion as diverse and individual on some topics and united on others; Indians are capable of changing their minds, and of coming independently to the same conclusions as the Anglo-Indian administrators. Duncan's refusal to "close" her definitions of races is exemplified in her article "Eurasia," published in 1892 in the American magazine *Popular Science Monthly*. The article begins in a clearly racist style by discussing the "racial type"[22] of the mixed Indian and European community, and identifying its characteristics, including colour, physique, accent, and moral character. Following the classic prejudice against the half-breed, she portrays the Eurasian as morally degenerate compared to either the European or the Indian, and describes the moral character as arising from physical degeneracy: "They seem to have a code of their own, which is capable of infinite infraction, and they touch a level of degradation which is far lower than any reached by the pure heathen about them. This is apparently an ineradicable thing, for it has its root in physical inheritance and its reason is racial" (6). How much of this obvious racism is attributable to Duncan's desire to sell an article to a magazine whose editorial policy was to publicize the views of the "social darwinists" is impossible to ascertain, yet her sympathy towards the Eurasian community, which was the object of economic and social discrimination, is clear.[23] Duncan rejects her own characterization of the Eurasian "racial type" in the last two paragraphs of the article. She acknowledges that prejudice limits her vision and the vision of other Europeans, and that much exists in common between all races: "Now that I have finished my imperfect sketch, the ink in which I have drawn it seems too black ... In the heart of Eurasia – a heart which has yet to be bared to us by the scalpel of modern fiction – surely may be found much that is worth adding to the grand total that makes humanity interesting. The article ends with a lyrical depiction of two pretty Eurasian girls promenading in the market with their mother, observed by "two very elegant young men, with dapper sticks and fresh ties" (9), implying that the essentials of life are the same for all races.

Duncan is aware of the difference of race in the context of her overall belief in the unity of humanity, just as she is aware of the uniqueness and legitimacy of nationality in the context of the ability of nations to interact to each others' benefit and to form alliances to promote peace. Canada is her ideal, but only because Canada's heritage allows Canadians to see more clearly their duty to help unite humanity and to discern the practical path towards that goal. Her path towards unity was, like that of many Canadians of her time, to "mend the broken teacup," to foster sentimental, political, and trade ties among colonies and former colonies of Britain, with a redistribution of power appropriate to the new prosperity and independence of member nations. Her view of the ideal Empire is of a union held together by familial sentiment – a view that presages the modern Commonwealth.

CHAPTER NINE

A "Colonial Edition"

The novels of Sara Jeannette Duncan question and challenge the view from the centre of Empire. They present a critique of the totalizing systems of materialism, bourgeois democracy, imperialism, and patriarchy by delineating the colonial point of view – the view from the margin, both part of and outside the central ideology. That point of view is informed by the idealism that many Canadian intellectuals saw as an antidote to the increasingly materialist view of both fiction and politics current in the US and Britain, and by the feminist advocacy that resisted the colonizing ideology of the patriarchal centre by expanding limited definitions of woman and of femininity.

Duncan's political views had their genesis in the idealism expressed by British and Canadian political and social writers of the last half of the nineteenth century. Matthew Arnold and, through him, Thomas Carlyle were the most important for Duncan. Through them and their Canadian interpreters, Duncan saw traditional society in Canada, England, the US, and India as threatened by the new values of materialism, scepticism, and political anarchy; in opposition to those values she saw idealism, heroism, and Arnoldian culture. While she depicts the forces of materialism as strong, her novels always imply the constant evolution of society towards the end predicted by Carlyle, when all humanity will see justice and the face of God.

The most important basic belief conveyed to Duncan through her reading was a kind of popular idealism[1] that pervaded Canadian intellectual life in the late nineteenth century. This popular version of the idealism of Carlyle and Arnold included a belief in transcendent and immutable values (which may or may not be identified with a christian God). These values might be approximated in human life by those with the gift of divining them (Carlyle's heroes) or through study of British history and its evolution towards the ideal. These values denied the claims of materialistic science to ultimate knowledge, kept alive the religious impulse through study of literature and religious traditions, and made fully human life (of whatever race or culture) the ultimate test of all technological innovation.

In Canada, idealism was the major philosophical tradition touching all levels of intellectual life in the last few decades of the nineteenth century. Carlylean ideas dominated education at all levels;[2] Arnold's works must have been familiar to educated readers of *The Week*, as Duncan could use his terms "philistines" and "culture" in her columns with no accompanying explanation. In addition, John Watson arrived in Canada in 1872, and his views dominated Canadian academic philosophy by the mid-1880s. His interpretation of Kantian idealism influenced Duncan's Presbyterian church and was the focus of debate in magazines such as *The Canadian Monthly and National Review*. Duncan's journalism and novels show the influence of all these streams of thought. Moreover, she shared the major idea common to Canadian idealists: support for a continued link between Canada and England as a bulwark against the rampant materialism and anarchic democracy that seemed to threaten from the south.

The idealism of Duncan's novels is distinctly unfashionable today. It is responsible, some say, for the repeated claim in the mid-twentieth century that Canada is still a "Victorian" society, out of step with the intellectual and artistic world; the part played by idealism in the justification of imperialist war and the arms race has made idealism and its trappings objects of well-earned revulsion. Yet Duncan's work implies that to abandon mutually agreed upon definitions of justice, truth, and compassion, to abandon the possibility of community, is to leave us open to the grossest violations of elementary human freedoms; the struggle for justice can be waged only by communities united by those common abstractions. While we may deplore Duncan's elitism, her racism, and her class consciousness, we may applaud and subscribe to her vision of a community united in its attempt to realize "justice and freedom and that sort of thing" in real life, through negotiation, affection, and sensitivity to other cultures.

The critique of democracy, and especially republican democracy, that is evident in Duncan's work comes directly from her idealism. Duncan depicts human beings as a complex of self-interest and self-transcendence; personal selfishness and common good constantly war in the characters she depicts. In her novels, simply giving the vote to more people does not necessarily ensure better government, because government is to be judged by a higher standard, not by the advantages it awards to interest groups. The issue of democracy is directly connected to social reform. The increasing triumph of materialist capitalism, which treats human beings as commodities, over traditional aristocratic responsibility for the poor made social reform a necessity for Britain; yet, in *The Consort*, giving the poor the vote, through which they could exact "revenge" upon the rich, seems to do little to ameliorate their problems. For Duncan, a meritocracy (which Carlyle defends in *Past and Present*) drawn from an independent, educated population is the solution that the colonies of Canada and Australia offer the British working poor.

The depiction of nationality in the novels is inevitably connected with Duncan's belief in the essential unity of English-speaking peoples, which she characterizes as the "Anglo-Saxon race." Although Canada, the United States, Britain, and India are unique nationalities formed by different histories and different physical and social conditions, they are linked by the common ideals of their British heritage and by ties of familial "sentiment." While the novels look forward to a re-unification of England and her colonies and former colonies, unique nationalities are not devalued in a drive for uniformity; the personal initiative of Americans, the traditions of Britons, the flexibility of Canadians, and the contemplative nationalism of Indians – all are legitimate points of view from which a prospective union would draw strength.

Canada is idealized in the novels for its ability to meld respect for British ideals with a unique North American belief in personal freedom. In *The Imperialist*, the citizens of Elgin, Ontario, are able to follow their "man of vision" toward an ideal future; while Lorne Murchison is defeated by corruption and self-interest, the ideal he represents persists in the history of the nation. This persistence of the British ideal in Canadian culture is even clearer in Mary Trent of *Cousin Cinderella* and Arthur Youghall of *His Royal Happiness*; both characters find their personal freedom and their vocation in helping to revitalize Britain's own sense of mission and strengthen her ties to the colonies.

The burgeoning nationalism of the "Canada First" era in Canadian political life, like the nationalism of the 1960s and 1970s, ran parallel to the beginnings of feminist organization and feminist action. While Duncan would not have called herself a feminist, her work disputed patriarchally imposed definitions of women's role and advocated importing the "feminine" values of affection, sentiment, negotiation, and connection into political life. She challenges the limited roles allowed to women by both social and literary convention in *A Social Departure* and, in her early journalism, encourages women to discard useless feminine weakness and to cultivate firmness of purpose. She redefines the traditional sentimental heroine in *Vernon's Aunt*, *The Simple Adventures of a Memsahib*, "A Mother in India," and other works, creating a protagonist who moves beyond the conventional narrative of love story and happy ending. She argues for giving women a role in political life through the ballot, as well as demonstrating in *Cousin Cinderella*, *The Consort*, and *The Burnt Offering* how women can participate in inter-cultural debates and, through marriage, choose to be actors in public life.

Duncan's novels show the relationship between countries to be a familial one, in which the feminine virtues of negotiation, connection, and affection are the most important in maintaining peace and harmony. In *The Burnt Offering*, India asks for "affection" from her British rulers; the enthusiasm of Lorne Murchison's "heart" favours closer ties within the Empire. Women themselves had a part to play in the international politics of empire: Helen Browne, Rani Janaki, Mary Trent, and other Duncan heroines offer a tangible way to promote love and sympathy among the countries of the Empire when they marry. In the idealist sense, these heroines find both personal identity and an important way to serve the best interest of the community in the fulfillment of their love.

Indian nationality is a melding of British and Indian elements in Duncan's novels. Duncan accepted the common justifications for the British rule of force in India: the good of the people, the benefits of education, and democratic reforms. Her Indian novels depict the future of India as a marriage between the best of India and England, formed through affection and compatible gifts. The novels focus on the workings of the Imperial Idea of social reform:

they contrast the gradual reforms of "culture," based on knowledge of the social situation and on general flexibility of mind as well as acquaintance with ideals, to the "Morrison's Pill" approach of attempting to enforce compliance with a single idea. The novels reveal Western education, dominated by science and scepticism, as a mixed blessing for a culture already closer to its God than the British.

The Indian novels also depict racial difference. Duncan's fictional method of creating "types," as well as the discourse of racism and orientalism, lead to her depiction of Indians as incapable of self-government. While she often displays her cultural ethnocentricity and regularly makes use of the negative stereotypes of Indians, she refuses to accept such stereotypes as final; her definitions of "others" are always open to redefinition and to possible alliance.

Duncan's novels are, finally, "colonial editions,"[3] which reproduce the aesthetic and political controversies common to the English-speaking world of her time from a Canadian and a female point of view. Her rejection of materialism in art and in its political forms of republican democracy, individualism, and the rule of "selfishness" reflects the general dominance of idealism in Canadian philosophy and literature long after the materialism and "psychologism" of modernism dominated elsewhere in the English-speaking world. She locates the centre of that materialism in the United States, which she depicts as losing its commitment to ideals in the War of Independence; her Americans provide a link between the cautionary tales of Thomas Chandler Haliburton and the plutocrats of Stephen Leacock. Duncan's Britons are less benign than Leacock's "Remarkable Uncle," because they retain enough power over Canadian foreign affairs for their ignorance to be threatening; yet, like the community-building Britons of John Richardson and Susanna Moodie, Duncan's Britons retain their status as inheritors of British values and still remain open to the influence of ideals. Canadians, as inheritors of both North American freedom and the cultural products of British evolution, are Duncan's ideal people. Common sense to the contrary, Canadians have responded to Lorne Murchison's call to community with other Canadians and within the Empire by reaffirming the country's "dominion status" and continuing to see the Commonwealth as an important forum for negotiation and for the achievement of social justice.

Anglo-Indian Terms

A.D.C.. Aide de camp. Duncan depicts these aides in the service of the Viceroy or the lieutenant governor as young, unmarried men whose primary duties were of a personal or social nature.

ANGLO-INDIAN. The usual term for Indian residents of English origin at the end of the nineteenth and beginning of the twentieth centuries.

ANNA. A coin worth one-sixteenth of a rupee.

AYAH. A female servant whose duties included care of children and acting as a lady's maid.

BABOO. Defined in the notes to "Eurasia" (*Popular Science Monthly*, November 1892) as a neutral term for male natives of Bengal, especially those employed as clerks. It is taken as equivalent to Mister in the columns of the *Indian Daily News*. It later became a term of abuse when used to address persons of some social or professional standing.

BAWARCHI. Cook.

BEARER. The head servant of the Anglo-Indian household, whose duties included supervising the other servants, handling the household accounts, and acting as a valet to the male head of the household.

BRAHMIN. A member of the highest or priestly caste in Hindu culture.

CHOTA MEM. Little Englishwoman, or Englishwoman who is low on the social scale in the Anglo-Indian community.

DAK-BUNGALOW. A small basic dwelling located at usual stopping places for the postal service. Provided by the government for the use of Anglo-Indian travellers. (Dak is the postal service.)

EURASIAN. A person of mixed "native" and European parentage, possibly a descendant of the Portuguese community.

JOHN COMPANY. The nickname for the East India Company, which administered India until 1857.

KITMUTGAR. A male servant who waits at table.

LAHK. One hundred thousand rupees.

MEMSAHIB. Wife of the sahib, or an English woman.

PICE, PIE. A coin worth one-twelfth of an anna.

PUNDIT, PUNDITA. A Hindu scholar, specializing in religion, philosophy, and literature.

PUNKAH. A large cloth fan which hung from the ceiling in most Anglo-Indian residences. The punkah was attached to a rope which usually threaded through a hole in the wall and hung down outside in a corridor where the punkah-wallah would pull it to insure that the fan was kept in motion. The familiar picture of the sahib at his ease, being fanned with a punkah, was often evoked to castigate Anglo-Indian luxury.

PURDAH. Literally, a curtain used to screen women from the gaze of men; the state of being secluded from all men except close relatives.

RYOT. A small tenant farmer.

SANYASI. The final step of brahmin life, which consists of renouncing material ease and becoming a religious beggar.

SUTTEE. A Hindu widow who immolates herself on the funeral pile with her husband's body; the immolation of a Hindu widow in this way.

SYCE. A servant employed to look after horses and drive the carriage. Also the driver of an Indian carriage for hire or ticca gharry.

TICCA GHARRY, GHARRY. A (usually) disreputable-looking carriage for hire, used by those Anglo-Indians who couldn't afford to keep their own carriages.

TOMMY. Short for Tommy Atkins, British private soldier. Usually depicted as uneducated, uncouth, and brutal.

UNCOVENANTED. An adjective applied to Englishmen living and working in India who do not work directly for the India Civil Service, but who are nonetheless public servants, such as teachers. The "uncovenanted ones" move in different social circles than the "covenanted" and do not have a government pension plan or death benefits which will accrue to their survivors.

WALLAH. Man. Often used in compound words, as in punkah-wallah.

ZENANA. The part of an Indian household reserved for women observing strict purdah.

Notes

1 See Howells, *Private and Fictional Words,* for discussion of connections between 1970s feminism and nationalism.
2 See the selection of Canadian political cartoons from the 1860s, 1870s and 1880s in Bengough, *A Caricature History of Canadian Politics.*
3 DuPlessis, *Writing Beyond the Ending,* 43.
4 Woolf, *A Room of One's Own,* 91.
5 DuPlessis, *Writing Beyond the Ending,* 33.
6 Tausky, *Novelist of Empire,* 153. Tausky cites Irving Howe's definition of the political novel: "The *idea* of society, as distinct from the mere unquestioned workings of society, has penetrated the consciousnesses of the characters in all of its profoundly problematic aspects, so that there is to be observed in their behaviour, and they are themselves often aware of, some coherent political loyalty or ideological identification."
7 Duncan uses the words America and American in different contexts to mean both the continent of North America and its inhabitants, and the United States and its inhabitants. To avoid confusion, I will use American or US to indicate the United States, and North American to indicate the continent.
8 Fowler, *Redney,* 284–5, 251.
9 Colby, *The Singular Anomaly,* 9.
10 DuPlessis, "For the Etruscans," 149.
11 DuPlessis, *Writing Beyond the Ending,* 33.

12 Lampman, "At the Mermaid Inn," in Davies, *At the Mermaid Inn*, 269.

13 Bissell, "Introduction," in Duncan, *The Imperialist*.

14 Stevenson, *Appraisals of Canadian Literature*, 126.

15 Frye, *The Bush Garden*, 237.

16 Peterman, "Humour and Balance in *The Imperialist*," 57–8.

17 Weir, "Towards a Feminist Hermeneutics," in Goddard, *Gynocritics*, 61.

18 For an extended discussion of romantic irony see Mellor, *English Romantic Irony*.

19 Armour and Trott, *Faces of Reason*, 222.

20 See Cook, *The Regenerators*.

21 McKillop, *A Disciplined Intelligence*, 196.

22 Haliburton, *Review of British Diplomacy and its Fruits*, passim.

23 Berger, *The Sense of Power*, 104.

24 Parkin quoted in Berger, *The Sense of Power*, 104.

25 Duncan, *His Royal Happiness*, 325.

26 Chodorow, *The Reproduction of Mothering*, 167 and passim; Gilligan, *In a Different Voice*, 7–8, 16–17.

27 Duncan, *The Simple Adventures of a Memsahib*, 10.

28 Lukacs, *The Historical Novel*, 254.

29 Mathews, *Canadian Literature*, 133; Armour and Trott, *Faces of Reason*, 319.

30 See Horowitz, "Introduction." For subsequent quotations see pages 13, 19, and 20.

31 Mathews, *Canadian Literature*, 28.

32 Berger, *The Sense of Power*, 177.

33 Quoted in Berger, *The Sense of Power*, 219.

34 See Roberts, "Rocking the Cradle for the World: The New Woman and Maternal Feminism" in Kealey, *A Not Unreasonable Claim*.

35 This study draws on Duncan's journalism to supplement or clarify many points discussed in relation to the novels. Most of Duncan's journalism is not simply reportage; while in Canada her contributions to *The Week*, *The Globe*, and the *Montreal Star* consisted mainly of columns of opinion on aesthetic, literary, or political matters, often pertaining to women. Her interviews and reports on exhibitions and other social occasions also contain liberal doses of authorial comment. Like many of her contemporaries, Duncan experimented with fictional narrative in her journalistic works, often blurring the distinction between the two. The integral rela-

tionship between her novels and her journalism has been demonstrated by Tausky (in *Novelist of Empire*), who uncovered many journalistic articles directly related to research she had undertaken for her novels. While in India, Duncan wrote editorials on political and social questions for the *Indian Daily News*, edited by her husband Everard Cotes, and contributed columns and stories to American magazines.

CHAPTER TWO

1 Weir, "Towards a Feminist Hermeneutics," in Goddard, *Gynocritics*, 61.
2 Ibid., 63.
3 See also Goddard, "Introduction," *Gynocritics*, v.
4 Weir, "Towards a Feminist Hermeneutics," in Goddard, *Gynocritics*, 68.
5 Showalter, *A Literature of Their Own*, 11.
6 In his article "A Special Tang," Watters also identifies irony as a particularly Canadian strategy, finding its source in our historical, economic, and political status. He quotes Lister Sinclair on the precarious position of Canada: "between the greatest and grimmest of the Grim Great Powers," (25) Canada has made self-preservation a fixed value in our humour, leading to "a kind of humour that combines full understanding of the contending forces with a wry recognition of one's ineffectiveness in controlling them" (26). Canadian irony is thus a self-protective gesture that allows colonials to have fun without "forgetting themselves in gay abandon" and to criticize without "losing their tempers in righteous wrath" (26).
7 Booth, *A Rhetoric of Irony*, 33.
8 Ibid., 28.
9 Ibid.
10 Tausky, *Novelist of Empire*, 77.
11 See, for example, Mellor, *English Romantic Irony*.
12 A summary of critical opinion on the seeming ambivalence of Duncan's authorial voice in *The Imperialist*, which seems to combine sympathy and satire, may be found in Zichy, "A Portrait of the Idealist as Politician," 342, n.2.
13 Duncan refers to Carlyle often in her journalism, e.g. *The Week*, 24 November 1887, 831; she characterizes the age as a self-conscious one (*The Week*, 3 March 1887, 216–7) following Carlyle in "Charac-

teristics"; she refers approvingly to hero-worship in *The Week*,
21 July 1887, 550–1. See chapter 3 for a discussion of Duncan's
idealism.

14 James, *The Art of The Novel*, 222.
15 Orthodocia identifies the narrator as S.J.D. (Sara Jeannette Duncan)
on page 175 of the novel.
16 Although a modern Canadian reader may disagree, the American
narrator is a "colonial" to Duncan by virtue of her relationship to
the imperial power from which the US sprang. Duncan's opinion of
this relationship may have changed in later life due to the
increasing militaristic belligerence of the US and the onset of the
First World War – see chapter 7.
17 The point of view is also important to Canadians in *The Imperialist*;
Lorne and his trade deputation keep their point of view while
attempting to influence British government policy and trade practices (see page 113).
18 Duncan, *The Imperialist*, 11. Compare with the discussion of occupation as a social indicator on page 47.
19 Cady, *The Light of Common Day*, chapter 1, passim.
20 See, for example, MacLennan, "Where is my Potted Palm?", 52.
21 See Nagarajan, "The Anglo-Indian Novels of Sara Jeannette
Duncan," 74, and Susanna Howe, *Novels of Empire*, 74–84.
22 Tausky, *Novelist of Empire*, 190.
23 "A Mother in India" is one of Duncan"s best-known stories and is
found in *The Pool in the Desert*.

CHAPTER THREE

1 Pacey, *Creative Writing in Canada*, 82.
2 MacLulich, "Novel and Romance," 46.
3 Tausky, *Novelist of Empire*, 73.
4 Fowler, *Redney*, 106.
5 Tausky, *Novelist of Empire*, 73.
6 Ibid., 73, 80.
7 Fowler, *Redney*, 106, 104; 106.
8 See discussion of the influence of Howells on Duncan in Tausky,
"The American Girls of William Dean Howells and Sara Jeannette
Duncan" and *Novelist of Empire*, chapters two, four and five, and in
Fowler, *Redney*, particularly 104–7.
9 W.P.C. in Ballstadt, *The Search for English Canadian Literature*, 12, 10.

10 McCulloch, *Letters of Mephibosheth Stepsure*, 134, 135, 136, 149.
11 Cady, *W.D. Howells as Critic*, 98. All further references to Howells's criticism are from this edition.
12 Roberts, "A Note on Russian Realism," 200. Duncan's poem "My Washerwoman's Story" appeared in the same issue.
13 Laura Groening's article on Susanna Moodie makes a similar point. Groening argues that Moodie's idealistic depiction of romantic nature is not a contradiction of the realism of *Roughing it in the Bush* and *Life in the Clearings*; for Moodie, idealism and realism are not incompatible, and the seeming dichotomy is "largely illusory, the results of a twentieth-century consciousness looking back on a nineteenth-century life." Groening, *"The Journals of Susanna Moodie"*, 167.
14 Leacock, "Fiction and Reality," 229.
15 Grove, *It Needs to be Said*, 61.
16 Duncan often refers to Carlyle often in her journalism, e.g., in *The Week*, 24 November 1887, 831. She characterizes the age as a self-conscious one (*The Week*, 3 March 1887, 216–17), following Carlyle in "Characteristics"; she refers approvingly to hero-worship in *The Week*, 21 July, 1887, 550–1. Rae Goodwin discusses Duncan's connection with Arnold in "The Early Journalism of Sara Jeannette Duncan, with a Chapter of Biography" 91–2; see also Tausky, *Novelist of Empire*, 278 and Fowler, *Redney*, 115 for Arnold connections.
17 Carlyle, *Sartor Resartus*, 54.
18 Duncan, *The Week*, 9 September 1886, 659.
19 Duncan's only direct statement on the reconcilation of the "idealities" of religion with the material world is an unsigned editorial in the *Indian Daily News* (4 December 1896) entitled "Theology and The Times," which may be attributed to her by internal evidence. The editorial laments the official acknowledgment by the Anglican church of the truth of Darwin's theory of evolution, and suggests that the church is "between the devil and the deep blue sea" in its attempt to seem both modern and stable. The editorial deplores the use of science to explore religious matters, and says of an attempt to use x-rays to discover the soul: "This is distasteful; we note its origin as American with satisfaction."
20 Her account of the distinctive ideas of nations follows Arnold's characterization of the powers of various nationalities: British conduct, Italian beauty, German knowledge, French manners. Duncan

continues by stating the characteristic idea of North America: "The most discoverable power in America so far seems to be the power of opportunity" ("Bric-a-Brac," *Montreal Star*, 14 February 1888, 2).

21 See Thomas, "Canadian Social Mythologies in Sara Jeannette Duncan's *The Imperialist*," 47. General comments on the influence of Carlyle on colonial writers appear in Howe, *Novels of Empire*, 66, 68, 73–5.

22 Allen, "Narrative Uncertainty in Duncan's *The Imperialist*," 48.

23 Duncan, *The Week*, 3 March 1887, 217.

24 Ibid., 7 October 1886, 723.

25 Ibid., 25 November 1886, 828.

26 James, "The Art of Fiction," *The Art of Fiction and other Essays*, 17.

27 Bissell, "Introduction," *The Imperialist*, ix.

28 Zezulka, "*The Imperialist*", 148, 149.

29 See the discussion of Graham Trent in Thomas, "Cousin Cinderella and the Empire Game," 183–93.

30 In this he resembles the hero of James's novel *Roderick Hudson*. See Dean, "A Note on *Cousin Cinderella* and *Roderick Hudson*," 96–8.

31 Alfred's nickname, "Cakes," refers to a well-known legend about King Alfred. According to the legend, Alfred hid from the Vikings in a peasant cottage, where the housewife suggested he make himself useful by keeping an eye on the cakes in the oven. Alfred got distracted, the cakes burned, and the housewife gave him a terrific scolding.

32 See my discussion of the relationship between the two in the introduction to the reprint of *A Daughter of Today* (1989).

33 See Tausky, chapters 2 and 4, and Fowler, esp. 104–7; also see Tausky, "The American Girls of William Dean Howells and Sara Jeannette Duncan."

34 Duncan, "Bric-a-Brac," *Montreal Star*, 5 December 1887, 2.

35 Cady, W.D. *Howells as Critic*, 122.

36 Ibid., 125.

37 Duncan, "Bric-a-Brac," *Montreal Star*, 5 December 1887, 2.

38 Ibid.

39 Duncan, *The Week*, 4 November 1886, 781.

40 Ibid., 15 July 1886, 553.

41 Ibid., 13 January 1887, 111, 112.

42 Allen, "Narrative Uncertainty in Duncan's *The Imperialist*."

43 Ibid., 53.

CHAPTER FOUR

1 Kealey, *A Not Unreasonable Claim*, 7.
2 Prentice, Bourne et al., *Canadian Women, A History*, 170.
3 Moers, *Literary Women*, 123.
4 Prentice, Bourne et al., *Canadian Women, A History*, 170.
5 See Roberts, "Rocking the Cradle for the World," in Kealey, *A Not Unreasonable Claim*.
6 Information on the new woman in Canada is available in Kealey, *A Not Unreasonable Claim*.
7 See, for example, Fowler, *Redney*, 18: "Advena Murchison is, in essence, Redney herself."
8 From an 1898 interview by Florence Donaldson published in *The Bookman*, quoted by Fowler in *Redney*, 235. Other biographical details from Fowler.
9 Identified by Fowler in *Redney*, 45.
10 Duncan, "Bric-a-Brac," *Montreal Star*, 28 January 1888, 4.
11 Ibid.
12 Duncan, "Other People and I," *The Globe*, 1 July 1885, 3.
13 Duncan's language of free market capitalism echoes the words of John Stuart Mill in his essay "The Subjection of Women," in which he argues that women must be left alone to determine their own vocations, because, "according to all the principles involved in modern society," individuals cannot be excluded by legislation from any means of livelihood. In his view, women will be prevented from taking on occupations for which they are unsuited by the principles of competition that operate in the free market: "What women by nature cannot do, it is quite superfluous to forbid them from doing. What they can do, but not so well as the men who are their competitors, competition suffices to exclude them from ... Whatever women's services are most wanted for, the free play of competition will hold out the strongest inducements to them to undertake." Duncan agrees with Mill that all professions should be opened to women on the principle that the free market will regulate the marketability of "woman-labour."
14 Duncan, "Saunterings," *The Week*, 2 December 1896, 6.
15 Duncan, "Afternoon Tea," *The Week*, 20 January 1887, 128.
16 Duncan, "Other People and I," *The Globe*, 1 July 1885, 3.
17 Ibid., 15 July 1885, 3. Duncan's insistence that women's names should mirror the dignity and the seriousness of their work throws

light on Fowler's citation of the several names with which Duncan signed her published work. Perhaps Duncan, too, was looking for a suitably professional name, as neutral as her earlier pseudonym Garth Grafton but expressive of her mature achievement without feminine frivolousness.

18 Ibid., 15 July 1885, 3.

19 Ibid., 23 May 1885, 6.

20 Ibid., 12 August 1885, 3.

21 Duncan, "Women Suffragists in Council," *The Week*, 25 March 1886, 261.

22 *Indian Daily News*, 8 June 1897; 25 February 1897.

23 Moers, *Literary Women*, 123.

24 Duncan, *The Simple Aventures of a Memsahib*, 107.

25 Defined in Moers, *Literary Women*, 122ff.

26 Duncan, "Outworn Literary Methods," *The Week*, 9 June 1887, 450–1.

27 See, for example, Mrs Hauksbee and Mrs Mallowe in Kipling, *In The Vernacular*.

28 Duncan, "A Mother in India," *The Pool in the Desert*, 2.

29 Contemporary accounts, including *The Englishwoman in India* by Maud Diver, characterize the Anglo-Indian wife as perpetually torn between her two roles.

30 Ross, "Calling Back the Ghost of the Old-Time Heroine," 46.

31 Duncan, "Saunterings," *The Week*, 16 August 1888, 603.

32 Ibid.

CHAPTER FIVE

1 For the reactions of other imperialists to democratic government, see Berger, *The Sense of Power*, 203–6.

2 Grant, *Ocean to Ocean*, 411.

3 Macdonald, "Speech in the Legislative Assembly on February 6, 1865," 32–3.

4 Grant, *Ocean to Ocean*, 410.

5 Duncan, "Saunterings," *The Week*, 17 March 1887, 249.

6 Smith, *Canada and the Canadian Question*, 254.

7 See Catherine Adams, "Introduction" to "An Annotated Edition of Sara Jeannette Duncan's Contributions to *The Week*."

8 Colquhoun, *Press, Politics and People*, 101.

9 Berger, *The Sense of Power*, 199.

10 Duncan, *Indian Daily News*, 14 August 1896, 4.

11 Ibid., 11 May 1896, 4.

12 Duncan, "The House of Lords of the Future," *Indian Daily News*, 6 May 1897, 4.

13 The influence of Ruskin might be traced more specifically in *Cousin Cinderella*. Graham Trent, who works in his father's lumber business, has a Ruskinite interest in craftsmanship. His sister describes him as "a kind of missionary in Minnebiac, of simple purposes and fine ideas in wood, the people there, though so near to nature's heart, being dreadfully fond of gilt and plush." Graham loves "the touch and the feeling and the idea of wood"; his carvings are like "a line of poetry, or a bar of music" (6). The civilizing influence of craftsmanship in industrial development extends symbolically to the workers at the sawmill; Graham makes a present of one of his finest pieces – "A mantelpiece ... with a design of fir trees" – to one of the foremen, who "thought a great deal of it" (6).

14 Disraeli, "General Preface," xiv.

15 Roberts, "The Beginnings of a Canadian Literature," *Selected Poetry and Critical Prose*, 246.

16 See Dean, "Canadian Nationality in the International Novels of Sara Jeannette Duncan."

17 Duncan, *The Week*, 14 October 1886, 739.

18 Ibid., 1 March 1888, 213–14.

19 Tausky believes Thakore is based on Bal Gangadhar Tilak, a religious nationalist leader who was imprisoned in 1897 and again in 1908. His newspaper, *Kesari*, was like Thakore's *Lamp of India* in its outspoken criticism of the British. See *Novelist of Empire*, 247–8. Thakore's name also resembles the surname of Rabindranath Tagore, a moderate nationalist politician and author, whom Duncan accused of being the author of seditious literature in the *Indian Daily News* (4 April 1897). Apparently, Duncan had not read any of Tagore's work, and she relied on a government publication on Bengali authors for her information on Tagore.

20 Mills is probably based on the Labour leader Kier Hardie. (See Tausky, *Novelist of Empire*, 247–8.)

21 Duncan personally favoured this reform. See *Indian Daily News*, 22 February 1897, 4, and Tausky, *Novelist of Empire*, 195.

22 Duncan, *Indian Daily News*, 14 September 1896, 4.

23 Ibid., 17 April 1896, 4.

24 See Berger, *The Sense of Power*, 141–2, 177–83, 191–3.

25 Tausky suggests that the Labour organizers in the novel are based on Beatrice and Sidney Webb (*Novelist of Empire*, 175).

26 Tausky, *Novelist of Empire*, 177. However, I question whether this emphasis is a new development in Duncan's work; see my discussion of *The Burnt Offering*, above.

27 Tausky, *Novelist of Empire*, 175.

28 Duncan, *On the Other Side of the Latch*, 68.

CHAPTER SIX

1 Duncan's depiction of the British Empire is discussed in Tausky, *Novelist of Empire*, passim; Fowler, *Redney*, 259, 280–1; and in articles by Catherine Adams, Peter Allen, A.G. Bailey, Diana Brydon, D.J. Dooley, Michael Peterman, Clara Thomas, and J.M. Zezulka. (See bibliography.)

2 Duncan, "South Africa and Cecil Rhodes," *Indian Daily News*, 17 February 1896, 4.

3 See, for example, Cook, "George R. Parkin and the Concept of Britannic Idealism."

4 Burke, "Speech on Fox's East India Bill, House of Commons, 1 December 1783," in Bennett, *The Concept of Empire from Burke to Attlee*, 51–2.

5 Islam, *Chronicles of the Raj*, 2.

6 Duncan, *Indian Daily News*, 11 December 1896, 4.

7 See Thornton, *The Imperial Idea and its Enemies*, 1–49.

8 Bailey, "The Historical Setting of Sara Duncan's *The Imperialist*," 71.

9 Haliburton, *Review of British Diplomacy and its Fruits*, 18–19.

10 See Berger, *The Sense of Power*, 100–1, for discussion of imperialist ideas about opposition between "selfishness" and "principles" among the Loyalists.

11 Ibid., 177.

12 Duncan, *The Week*, 2 September 1886, 643.

13 Berger, *The Sense of Power*, passim.

14 The *Indian Daily News* favourably quotes a speech by Joseph Chamberlain on imperial federation, in which he looks forward to an alliance of equal nations: "The attitude of superior toward inferior has been replaced by a sense of equal kinship, and that may give place, by and by, to a closer union still" (21 April 1897). Imperial federation did have some support in England; the Imperial Federation League was begun there in 1884. But the idea of the Empire as

a group of independent but associated nations originated in Canada, and has had a much more lasting effect in Canadian political and intellectual life than have similar ideas in Britain.

15 Useful discussions of imperialism in the novel appear in, among others, Allen, "Narrative Uncertainty in Duncan's *The Imperialist*," Bailey, "The Historical Setting of Sara Duncan's *The Imperialist*," Tausky, *Novelist of Empire*, 153–74, and Thomas, "Canadian Social Mythologies in Sara Jeannette Duncan's *The Imperialist*."

16 Duncan also refers to chivalry and medieval knights in her descriptions of Lord Doleford in *Cousin Cinderella*, of Prince Alfred in *His Royal Happiness*, and of Roddy Trenchard in *The Gold Cure*.

17 Dean, "Duncan's Representative Men," 117–19.

18 This incident is probably based on two similar cases during the viceroyalty of George Nathaniel Curzon; see Edwardes, *The High Noon of Empire*, 85–7, 167.

CHAPTER SEVEN

1 Duncan, "Books of the Week," *Indian Daily News*, 22 August 1896, 5.

2 "German vs British trade," *Indian Daily News*, 9 September, 1896. According to the cited article, Germany rivalled England in only a few manufacturing sectors, including glassware. This may be the source of Mr Chafe's worries about German competition in *The Imperialist*, 119. A passage quoted from *Made In Germany* in the earlier review bears a striking resemblance to the famous passage pointing out the extent of Canadian trade with the US: see *The Imperialist*, 128.

3 *Indian Daily News*, 20 June 1896, 4.

4 Duncan, "Cleveland and Cuba," *Indian Daily News*, 25 March 1896, 4.

5 Duncan, "Voices in the Wilderness," *Indian Daily News*, 12 June 1896, 4.

6 Levitt, "Race and Nation," 4. For Berger see *The Sense of Power*, 92–3.

7 From this view of Canada grew the now-familiar role of Canada as peacemaker in world politics.

8 See Hofstader, *Social Darwinism in American Thought*, 174 for reference to James K. Hosmer's *Short History of Anglo-Saxon Freedom*, for example.

9 Hofstader, *Social Darwinism in American Thought*, 175; Roosevelt,

"Biological Analogies in History" in Darwin, *The Descent of Man*, 512–19.

10 Hofstader, *Social Darwinism in American Thought*, 170ff.
11 Cook, "George R. Parkin and the Concept of Britannic Idealism," 19.
12 Parkin, *Imperial Federation*, 57.
13 Darwin, *The Descent of Man*, 269.
14 Parkin, *Imperial Federation*, 1.
15 Lampman, "From Two Canadian Poets," in Daymond and Monkman, *Towards a Canadian Literature* I, 134, 135.
16 Berger, *The Sense of Power*, 128–30.
17 Duncan, *The Week*, 2 September 1886, 643.
18 Duncan, "American Influence on Canadian Thought," in Daymond and Monkman, *Towards a Canadian Literature* I, 119.
19 Ibid.
20 "Bric-a-Brac," *Montreal Star*, 14 February 1888, 2.
21 Duncan may have shared the ideas of Goldwin Smith, editor of *The Week*, who expressed his view of the similarity of Canadian and American character in *Canada and the Canadian Question* (1891). He presents Americans and Canadians as essentially democratic peoples, wholly alike in reverencing British aristocrats out of "personal habit": "Americans and Canadians are in this respect the same ... Canadian sentiment may be free from the revolutionary tinge and the tendency to indiscriminate sympathy with the rebellion contracted by American sympathy in the contest with George III; but it is not less thoroughly democratic" (27). Duncan's view of Canadians as "democrats who had never thrown off the monarch" is comparable to Smith's. For Smith, however, the common democracy draws the two nationalities together, while for Duncan the preservation of monarchy in Canada is a vital difference.
22 "The Thorns of Diplomacy," *Indian Daily News*, 11 May 1896, 4.
23 See Tausky, *Novelist of Empire*, 94; also "The American Girls of William Dean Howells and Sara Jeannette Duncan," 146–58.
24 The following account of the relationships between freedom and tradition in Duncan's novels contains the essential ideas developed in my thesis "Canadian Nationality in the International Novels of Sara Jeannette Duncan."
25 Berger, *The Sense of Power*, 162.
26 Beveridge quoted in Hofstader, *Social Darwinism*, 182.
27 Tausky, *Novelist of Empire*, 146.

28 Duncan, *The Week*, 23 September 1886, 691.

29 Through the efforts of Dr Carl F. Klinck, a collection of the twelve plays in Sara Jeannette Duncan's possession at the time of her death in 1922 has been deposited in the D.B. Weldon Library at the University of Western Ontario. The plays are typed, enclosed in folders bearing the business cards of various commercial typists in London, and corrected in pencil and ink in more than one hand, one of which is certainly Duncan's. Some are dated, and others can be dated by accompanying press clippings giving accounts of various performances. Two are dramatic versions of stories later published in novel form: *Title Clear* (1922) and *The Gold Cure* (1924). Most are specifically concerned with the war effort.

Additional plays in the collection include *A Lady in the Case* (by Paul Kester, inscribed on the cover "Property of Annie Russell") and *Molly Mary*, which was evidently left unfinished, and is accompanied by several pages of typed notes and handwritten suggestions from Everard Cotes on how the play might be completed.

30 See Tausky, *Novelist of Empire*, 274.

31 Two versions of *Julyann* are included in the collection, one in four acts and one in three. The four-act version has a first act which is substantially rewritten in the three-act version; otherwise the two are nearly identical, with the original acts 3 and 4 becoming act 3, scenes one and two. Quotations are from the four-act version.

CHAPTER EIGHT

1 Said, *Orientalism*, 227.

2 Ibid., 205.

3 Duncan, "Eurasia," 9.

4 Darwin, *The Descent of Man*, 266.

5 Hofstader, *Social Darwinism in American Thought*, 171.

6 The Canadian reaction to Darwinism is documented in Ramsay Cook, *The Regenerators*, and McKillop, *A Disciplined Intelligence*; for the us reaction, see Hofstader, *Social Darwinism in American Thought*, and Anderson, *Race and Rapprochement*; British application of Darwin to social issues is discussed in Jones, *Social Darwinism and English Thought*.

7 "A Friend to be Saved From," *Indian Daily News*, 18 April 1896.

8 *Indian Daily News*, 28 April 1896. A reference in this editorial to North American Indians seems to identify it as Duncan's work.

9 An editorial that appeared in the *Indian Daily News* during Duncan's tenure laments the Anglican church's official acceptance of Darwinian evolution and suggests that such scientific theories create unresolvable difficulties for the spiritually minded ("Theology and the Times," 4 December 1896).

10 Duncan, "Slavery and Famine,", *Indian Daily News*, 15 February 1897, 4.

11 Duncan, *Indian Daily News*, 23 October 1896, 4.

12 *Indian Daily News*, 5 May 1897, 4.

13 Duncan, *Indian Daily News*, 3 April 1897, 4.

14 *Indian Daily News*, 22 February 1896, 4.

15 This chapter may be the source of E.M. Forster's famous opening chapter in *A Passage to India*, in which he gives a remarkably similar account contrasting English and Indian communities. Forster visited Duncan in Simla in 1912, six years after the publication of *Set In Authority*; it is tempting to speculate that Forster had read the book, if only as a compliment to his hostess.

16 In *The Story of Sonny Sahib*, Duncan makes eloquence and tradition (and perhaps lying) the essence of Indian culture when she says Sonny's Indian friends excel in storytelling: "It was the single thing they could do better than he did" (24).

17 Michael Edwardes's *British India* might stand as an example of this school of thought.

18 See Tausky, *Novelist of Empire*, 258–9 for examples.

19 Duncan, "In a Far Country," *Indian Daily News*, 15 April 1896.

20 Mary Louise Pratt defines the term in "Scratches on the Face of the Country; or, What Mr Barrow saw in the Land of the Bushmen," 120: "The people to be othered are homogenized into a collective 'they.'" The term might also be used to describe Duncan's creation of "insiders" and "outsiders" through colonial irony – see chapter 2.

21 In addition to examples given previously, see the discussion of the international novel in MacMillan, "The Maritime Novel," 25–32.

22 Duncan, "Eurasia," 1.

23 See also Fowler, *Redney*, 214.

CHAPTER NINE

1 Defined by Terry Cook in "George R. Parkin."
2 Thomas, "Canadian Social Mythologies in Sara Jeannette Duncan's *The Imperialist*," 47.
3 British publishers produced colonial editions for circulation in the colonies. In *Cousin Cinderella*, Senator Trent calls Graham and Mary Trent "a pair of colonial editions" when he is deciding to send them to England to gain sophistication.

Bibliography

WORKS BY DUNCAN

Columns

The Globe. "Other People and I." May 1885 to September 1885. "Woman's
 World." September 1886 to April 1887.
Montreal Star. "Bric-a-Brac." November 1887 to November 1888.
The Week. "Saunterings," "Afternoon Tea." February 1886 to September 1888.

Articles

"The Dignity of Prince Rupert." *The Globe,* 4 October 1919, 14.
"Eurasia." *Popular Science Monthly* 42, no. 1 (November 1892): 1–9.
"The Heir Apparent." *Harper's Monthly* 110 (March 1905): 625–31.
"The Home Life of Lady Curzon." *Harper's Bazaar* 37 (March 1903): 222–24.
"Little Windows of a Dynasty." *Harper's Monthly* 104 (December 1902): 115–
 21.
"The Melting Pot Bubbles a Bit." *The Globe,* 13 October 1919, 5.
"The Ordination of Asoka." *Harper's Monthly* 105 (October 1902): 753–9.
The Indian Daily News. Editorials and book reviews. 1896 to 1897.
Selected Journalism. Edited by Thomas Tausky. Ottawa: Tecumseh Press, 1978.

Novels

An American Girl in London. New York: D. Appleton, 1891.
The Burnt Offering. 1910. Reprint. Toronto: University of Toronto Press, 1978.
The Consort. 1912. Reprint. Toronto: University of Toronto Press, 1978.
Cousin Cinderella. 1908. Reprint. Toronto: University of Toronto Press, 1980.

A Daughter of Today. 1895. Reprint. Ottawa: The Tecumseh Press, 1988.

The Gold Cure. London: Hutchinson, 1924.

His Honor, and a Lady. New York: D. Appleton, 1896.

His Royal Happiness. Toronto: Hodder and Stoughton, 1914.

The Imperialist. 1904. Reprint. Toronto: McClelland and Stewart, 1971.

On the Other Side of the Latch. London: Methuen, 1901.

The Path of a Star. Toronto: W.J. Gage, 1899.

The Pool in the Desert. 1903. Reprint. Harmondsworth: Penguin, 1984.

Set in Authority. New York: Doubleday Page and Co., 1906.

The Simple Adventures of a Memsahib. New York: D. Appleton, 1893.

A Social Departure. New York: D. Appleton, 1890.

The Story of Sonny Sahib. London: Macmillan and Co., 1894.

Title Clear. London: Hutchinson and Co., n.d. [1922].

Those Delightful Americans. New York: D. Appleton, 1902.

Two Girls on a Barge [V. Cecil Cotes, pseud.]. London: Chatto and Windus, 1891.

Two in a Flat [Jane Wintergreen, pseud.]. London: Hodder and Stoughton [1908].

Vernon's Aunt. London: Chatto and Windus, 1894.

A Voyage of Consolation. New York: D. Appleton, 1898.

Plays

Manuscripts of plays by Duncan are in the collection of the D.B. Weldon Library, University of Western Ontario.

SECONDARY SOURCES

Adams, Catherine. "An Annotated Edition of Sara Jeannette Duncan's Contributions to *The Week*." Master's thesis, Carleton University, 1980.

Allen, Grant. *The Woman Who Did.* Boston: Little, Brown, 1926.

Allen, Peter. "Narrative Uncertainty in Duncan's *The Imperialist*." *Studies in Canadian Literature* 9, no. 1 (1984): 41–60.

Anderson, Stuart. *Race and Rapprochement.* New Jersey: Associated University Presses, 1981.

Anon. "Fiction." Review of *Set in Authority*. *Times Literary Supplement*, 25 May 1906, 192.

Armour, Leslie and Trott, Elizabeth. *Faces of Reason.* Waterloo: Wilfred Laurier University Press, 1981.

Arnold, Matthew. "Democracy." *Complete Prose Works*, ed. R.H. Super. Ann Arbour: University of Michigan Press, 1962.

– *Poetry and Criticism of Matthew Arnold*, ed. Dwight Culler. Boston: Houghton Mifflin, 1961.

Bailey, A.G. "The Historical Setting of Sara Duncan's *The Imperialist.*" *Twentieth-Century Essays on Confederation Literature*, ed. L. McMullen. Ottawa: Tecumseh Press, 1976.

Ballstadt, Carl, ed. *The Search for English Canadian Literature*. Toronto: University of Toronto Press, 1975.

Beauchamp, Marie Annette. *Elizabeth and her German Garden*. London: Methuen, 1898.

Bengough, J.W. *A Caricature History of Canadian Politics*. 1886. Reprint. Toronto: Peter Martin Assoc., 1974.

Bennett, George, ed. *The Concept of Empire from Burke to Attlee*. London: Adam and Charles Black, 1962.

Berger, Carl. *The Sense of Power*. Toronto: University of Toronto, 1971.

Booth, Wayne. "A New Strategy for Establishing a Truly Democratic Criticism." *Dedalus, Reading Old and New* 112, no. 1 (Winter 1983): 193–214.

– *A Rhetoric of Irony*. Chicago: University of Chicago Press, 1974.

Boumela, Penny. *Thomas Hardy and Women*. Wisconsin: University of Wisconsin Press, 1985.

Brydon, Diana. "The Colonial Heroine." *Canadian Literature* 86 (Autumn 1980): 41–8.

Buckler, William, ed. *Prose of the Victorian Period*. Boston: Houghton Mifflin, 1958.

Cady, Edwin. *The Light of Common Day*. Bloomington: Indiana University Press, 1971.

– ed. *W.D. Howells as Critic*. Boston: Routledge and Kegan Paul, 1973.

Carlyle, Thomas. *Past and Present*. New York: Dutton, 1912.

– *Sartor Resartus* and *On Heroes and Hero Worship*. New York: Dutton, 1973.

Charlesworth, Hector. "The Canadian Girl." *Canadian Magazine* (May 1893): 186–93.

Chodorow, Nancy. *The Reproduction of Mothering*. Berkley: University of California Press, 1978.

Colby, Vineta. *The Singular Anomaly: Women Novelists of the Nineteenth Century*. New York: New York University Press, 1970.

Colquhoun, A.H. *Press, Politics and People: The Life and Letters of Sir John Willison*. Toronto: Macmillan, 1935.

Cook, Ramsay. *The Regenerators: Social Criticism in Late Victorian English Canada*. Toronto: University of Toronto Press, 1985.

Cook, Terry. "George R. Parkin and the Concept of Britannic Idealism." *Journal of Canadian Studies* 10, no. 3 (August 1975): 15–31.

Cowasjee, Saros, ed. *Stories from the Raj: from Kipling to Independence*. London: Bodley head, 1982.

Darwin, Charles. *The Descent of Man* in *Darwin*, edited by Philip Appleman. New York: W.W. Norton and Co., 1970.

Davies, Barrie, ed. *At the Mermaid Inn*. Toronto: University of Toronto Press, 1979.

Daymond, Douglas and Monkman, Leslie, ed. *Towards a Canadian Literature*. 2 vols. Ottawa: Tecumseh, 1984.

Dean, Misao. "Canadian Nationality in the International Novels of Sara Jeannette Duncan: Growing Goldenrod in Simla." Master's thesis, Carleton University, 1982.

– "Duncan's Representative Men." *Canadian Literature* 98 (Autumn 1983): 117–19.

– "A Note on *Cousin Cinderella* and *Roderick Hudson*." *Studies in Canadian Literature* 11, no. 1 (Spring 1986): 96–8.

– "Political Change in Sara Jeannette Duncan's Novels." *The Literary Criterion* 29, nos. 3–4 (1984): 93–104.

– "The Process of Definition: Canadian Nationality in the Early International Novels of Sara Jeannette Duncan." *Journal of Canadian Studies* 20, no. 2 (September 1985): 132–49.

Dewart, Edward Hartley, ed. *Selections from Canadian Poets*. 1864. Reprint. Toronto: University of Toronto Press, 1973.

Disraeli, Benjamin. "General Preface." *The Collected Works of the Right Hon. Benjamin Disraeli*. New Edition. London: Longman's, Green and Co., 1870.

Diver, Katherine Helen Maude (Marshall). *Siege Perilous and other Stories*. 1924. Reprint. New York: Books for Libraries Press, 1970.

Donaldson, Florence. "Mrs. Everard Cotes (Sara Jeannette Duncan)." *The Bookman* 14 (June 1898): 65–7.

Dooley, D.J. "Sara Jeannette Duncan: Political Morality at the Grass Roots." *Moral Vision in the Canadian Novel*, 25–35. Toronto: Clarke Irwin, 1979.

DuPlessis, Rachel Blau. "For the Etruscans." *The Future of Difference*, ed. Eisenstein and Jardine. Boston: G.K. Hall, 1980.

– *Writing Beyond the Ending*. Bloomington: University of Indiana Press, 1985.

Edwardes, Michael. *Bound to Exile*. London: Sidgewick and Jackson, 1969.

– *British India*. New York: Taplinger Publishing, 1968.

– *The High Noon of Empire*. London: Eyre and Spottiswoode, 1965.

Fish, Stanley. "Short People Have No Reason to Live." *Dedalus, Reading Old and New* 112, no. 1 (Winter 1983): 175–92.

Forster, E.M. *Selected Letters*, ed. Mary Lago and P.N. Furbank. London: Arrow Books, 1983.

Foster, Shirley. *Victorian Women's Fiction: Marriage, Freedom and the Individual.* London: Croom Helm, 1985.

Fowler, Marian. *Redney: A Life of Sara Jeannette Duncan.* Toronto: Anansi, 1983.

Frye, Northrop. *The Bush Garden.* Toronto: Anansi, 1971.

Gerson, Carole. "Duncan's Web." *Canadian Literature* 63 (Winter 1975): 73–80.

– "Speculations." Review of *Redney*, by Marian Fowler. *Canadian Literature* 103 (Winter 1984): 78–80.

Gilligan, Carole. *In a Different Voice.* Cambridge: Harvard University Press, 1982.

Goddard, Barbara. "A Portrait with Three Faces: The New Woman in Fiction by Canadian Women, 1880 – 1920." *The Literary Criterion* 19, nos. 3–4 (1984): 72–92.

– ed. *Gynocritics.* Toronto: ECW Press, 1987.

Goodwin, Rae. [Rae Goodwin Storey] "The Early Journalism of Sara Jeannette Duncan, with a Chapter of Biography." Master's thesis, University of Toronto, 1964.

Grant, G. M. *Ocean to Ocean.* Revised Edition. Toronto: Radisson Society, 1925.

Groening, Laura. "*The Journals of Susanna Moodie*: A Twentieth-Century look at a Nineteenth-Century Life." *Studies In Canadian Literature* 8, no. 2 (1983): 166–80.

Grove, Frederick Philip. *It Needs to be Said.* Toronto: Macmillan, 1929.

Haliburton, Robert Grant. *Review of British Diplomacy and its Fruits.* London: Samson, Low, Marston, Low and Searle, 1872.

Heilbrun, Carolyn. *Reinventing Womanhood.* New York: Norton, 1979.

Hill, Claudia. "The Imperial Idea in the novels of Ralph Connor and Sara Jeannette Duncan." Master's thesis, University of Toronto, 1964.

Hofstader, Richard. *Social Darwinism in American Thought.* Boston: Beacon Press, 1955.

Horowitz, Gad. "Introduction." *Canadian Labour in Politics.* Toronto: University of Toronto Press, 1971.

Howe, Susanna. *Novels of Empire.* New York: Columbia University Press, 1949.

Howells, Coral Ann. *Private and Fictional Words.* London: Methuen, 1987.

Islam, Shamsul. *Chronicles of the Raj.* London: Macmillan, 1979.

James, Henry. *The Art of Fiction and Other Essays.* New York: Oxford University Press, 1948.

– *The Art of The Novel.* New York: Charles Scribner's Sons, 1934.

– *Roderick Hudson.* 1908. Reprint. London: Oxford University Press, 1980.

Jones, Greta. *Social Darwinism and English Thought.* Sussex: Harvester Press, 1980.

Kealey, Linda, ed. *A Not Unreasonable Claim : Women and Reform in Canada, 1880s to 1920.* Toronto: The Women's Press, 1979.

Kipling, Rudyard. *In the Vernacular: The English in India,* ed. Randall Jarrell. New York: Doubleday, 1963.

– *Rudyard Kipling's Verse, Definitive Edition.* New York: Doubleday, 1940.

Leacock, Stephen. *Essays and Literary Studies.* New York: John Lane, 1916.

Levitt, Joseph. "Race and Nation in Canadian Anglophone Historiography." *Canadian Review of Studies in Nationalism* 8, no. 1 (Spring 1981): 1–16.

– *A Vision Beyond Reach.* Ottawa: Deneau, 1982.

Lukacs, George. *The Historical Novel.* Translated by Hannah and Stanley Mitchell. London: Merlin Press, 1963.

– *The Meaning of Contemporary Realism.* Translated by John and Necke Mander. London: Merlin Press, 1963.

McCulloch, Thomas. *The Letters of Mephibosheth Stepsure.* Toronto: McClelland and Stewart, 1960.

Macdonald, John A. "Speech in the Legislative Assembly, February 6, 1865." *Parliamentary Debates on the Confederation of the British North American Provinces.* 1865. Reprint. Ottawa: The Queen's Printer, 1951: 32–3.

McKenna, Isobel. "Sara Jeannette Duncan: The New Woman. A Critical Biography." Ph.D. diss., Queen's University, 1980.

– "Women in Canadian Literature." *Canadian Literature* 62 (Autumn 1974): 69–78.

McKillop, A.B. "John Watson and the Idealist Legacy." *Canadian Literature* 83 (Winter 1979): 72–89.

– *A Disciplined Intelligence.* Montreal: McGill-Queen's University Press, 1979.

MacLennan, Hugh. "Where is my Potted Palm?" *Thirty and Three,* ed. Dorothy Duncan. Toronto: Macmillan, 1954.

MacLulich, T.D. "L.M. Montgomery's Portraits of the Artist: Realism, Idealism and the Romantic Imagination." *English Studies in Canada* 11, no. 4 (December 1985): 459–73.

– "Novel and Romance." *Canadian Literature* 70 (August 1976): 42–50.

– *Between Europe and America: The Canadian Tradition in Fiction.* Toronto: ECW Press, 1988.

MacMillan, Carrie. "The Maritime Novel." *Studies in Canadian Literature* 11, no. 1 (Spring 1986): 19–37.

Mair, Charles. *Dreamland and Other Poems.* 1868. Reprint. Toronto: University of Toronto Press, 1974.

Mathews, Robin. *Canadian Literature, Surrender or Revolution.* Toronto: Steel Rail Publishing, 1978.

Matthews, John. "Literature and Politics, a Disraelian View." *English Studies in Canada* 10, no. 2 (June 1984): 172–87.

Mellor, Anne K. *English Romantic Irony*. Cambridge: Harvard University Press, 1980.

Mill, John Stuart. *On Liberty*, ed. Elizabeth Rapaport. Indianapolis: Hackett Publishing, 1978.

– *The Subjection of Women*. New York: Dutton, 1929.

Millett, Kate. *Sexual Politics*. New York: Doubleday, 1970.

Moers, Ellen. *Literary Women: The Great Writers*. New York: Oxford University Press, 1979.

Morton, Elizabeth. "Religion in Elgin: A Re-evaluation of the Subplot of *The Imperialist* by Sara Jeannette Duncan." *Studies in Canadian Literature* 11, no. 1 (Spring 1986): 99–107.

Moss, John. "Colonial Isolation." *Patterns of Isolation in English Canadian Fiction*. Toronto: McClelland and Stewart, 1974: 53–79.

Murray, Louisa. "Democracy in Literature." *The Week*, 2 August 1889, 550.

Nagarajan, S. "The Anglo-Indian Novels of Sara Jeannette Duncan." *Journal of Canadian Fiction* 3, no. 4 (1975): 74–84.

Pacey, Desmond. *Creative Writing in Canada*. 1961. Reprint. Connecticut: The Greenwood Press, 1976.

Parkin, George. *Imperial Federation*. London: Macmillan and Co., 1892.

– *The Great Dominion*. London: Macmillan and Co., 1895.

Peterman, Michael. "Humour and Balance in *The Imperialist*." *Journal of Canadian Studies* 11, no. 2 (May 1976): 56–64.

Pratt, Mary Louise. "Scratches on the Face of the Country; or, What Mr. Barrow saw in the Land of the Bushmen." *Critical Inquiry* 12, no. 1 (Autumn 1985): 119–43.

Prentice, Bourne et al. *Canadian Women, A History*. Toronto: Harcourt Brace Jovanovitch, 1988.

Roberts, Charles G.D. "A Note on Russian Realism." *The Week*, 23 February 1888, 200.

– *Selected Poetry and Critical Prose*, ed. W.J. Keith. Toronto: University of Toronto Press, 1974.

Ross, Catharine Sheldrick. "Calling Back the Ghost of the Old Time Heroine: Duncan, Montgomery, Atwood, Laurence, Munro." *Studies in Canadian Literature* 4, no. 1 (Winter 1979): 43–58.

Ruskin, John. *Sesame and Lilies*. 1891. Reprint. Michigan: Scholar Press, 1972.

Said, Edward. *Orientalism*. New York: Random House, 1979.

Showalter, Elaine. *A Literature of Their Own*. Princeton: Princeton University Press, 1977.

Singh, Bhupal. *A Survey of Anglo-Indian Fiction*. 1934. Reprint. London: Curzon Press, 1974.

Slonim, Leon. "Character, Action and Theme in *The Imperialist*." *Essays on Canadian Writing* 3 (Winter 1966): pp. 15–19.

Smith, Allan. "The Thought of G.M. Grant." *Canadian Literature* 83 (Winter 1979): 90–117.

Smith, Goldwin. *Canada and the Canadian Question*. Toronto: Hunter Rose and Co., 1891.

Smyth, Donna. *Subversive Elements*. Toronto: The Women's Press, 1986.

Spear, Perceval. *Penguin History of India*. Vol. 2. London: Penguin, 1956.

Stevenson, Lionel. *Appraisals of Canadian Literature*. Toronto: Macmillan, 1926.

Tausky, Thomas. "The American Girls of William Dean Howells and Sara Jeannette Duncan." *Journal of Canadian Fiction* 13 (1975): 146–58.

– "The Citizenship of Elfrida Bell." *Canadian Literature* 63 (Winter 1975): 127–8.

– "Duncan's Passage to India." *Canadian Literature* 73 (Summer 1977): 33–53.

– *Sara Jeannette Duncan, Novelist of Empire*. Port Credit: P.D. Meaney, 1980.

Thomas, Clara. "Cousin Cinderella and the Empire Game." *Studies in Canadian Literature* 1, no. 2 (Summer 1976): 183–93.

– "Canadian Social Mythologies in Sara Jeannette Duncan's *The Imperialist*." *Journal of Canadian Studies* 12, no. 2 (Summer 1976): 38–49.

– Review of *Sara Jeannette Duncan, Novelist of Empire* and *Annie Howells and Achille Frechette*. *English Studies in Canada* 8, no. 1 (March 1982): 103–8.

Thornton, A.P. *The Imperial Idea and its Enemies*. London: Macmillan, 1959.

Vauthier, Simone. "Sara Jeannette Duncan's 'A Mother in India.'" *Canadian Woman Studies* 6, no. 1 (Fall 1984): 101–2.

Watters, R.E. "A Special Tang: Stephen Leacock's Canadian Humour." *Canadian Literature* 5 (Summer 1960): 21–32.

Ward, Mary Augusta. *Robert Ellsmere*. 3 vols. London: Smith, Elder and Co., 1888.

– *Canadian Born*. London: Smith Elder and Co., 1910.

Woodcock, George. "Nostalgic Repetitions." *Canadian Literature* 98 (Autumn 1983): 116–17.

Woolf, Virginia. *A Room of One's Own* and *Three Guineas*. London: The Hogarth Press, 1984.

Zezulka, J.M. "*The Imperialist* :Imperialism, Provincialism, and Point of View." *Beginnings: A Critical Anthology*, ed. John Moss. Toronto: NC Press, 1980, 143–57.

– "Passionate Provincials: Imperialism, Regionalism and Point of View." *Journal of Canadian Fiction* 22 (1978): 80–92.

Zichy, Francis. "A Portrait of the Idealist as Politican: The Individual and Society in *The Imperialist*." *English Studies in Canada* 10, no. 3 (September 1984): 330–42.

– "Sara Jeannette Duncan." *Profiles in Canadian Literature*, ed. Jeffrey Heath. Toronto, Dundurn, 1980: 33–40.

Index

Adam, Graeme Mercer, 52–3
Alaska Panhandle dispute, 101
American Revolutionary War, 80, 122
Anglo-American tribunal, 121
Anglo-India. *See* India
Anglo-Indian point of view, 5, 14, 33, 107
Anglo-Saxon race, 101, 122–4, 126, 131, 156; and British Empire, 138–9; and US, 125,129–30, 131–2, 137
Arnold, Matthew, 4, 15, 46, 51, 86, 109, 154, 155

Barr, Robert, 126
Boer War, 140
British Empire, 4–5, 14, 101–20, 147; and agriculture, 104–5; British theories of, 104–8; Canadian ambivalence toward, 6, 101, 108, 114; conflict with local interests, 10–12, 107, 108, 113–14, 116–19; family metaphor, 13, 80, 102–3, 114, 153; and idealism, 4–5, 53, 102, 109, 155; Indian hostility to, 142–3; mission of, 102, 106, 111;

and US, 80, 107, 108, 120, 121, 122, 125. *See also* Femininity and British Empire, Idealism, Loyalty to British crown, Marriage metaphor
British nationality, 126, 128
Burke, Edmund, 44, 104, 141

Canada, 3–4, 5, 15–16, 20, 27–8, 29–33, 41, 79–80, 81, 82, 87–9, 90, 100, 101, 104, 107–9, 111–16, 121, 122–3, 124, 125, 126, 127, 128–9, 130, 136, 139, 150–1; as agricultural, 79, 104, 113; as feminine, 5, 102, 103; French, 150–1; as mediator, 122–3, 129–32; 136; as social ideal, 87–8, 89, 128–9, 153, 156
Canada First movement, 15, 83, 108
Canadian critique of Britain, 88–9
Canadian critique of US, 80, 127–8
Canadian nationalism, 122–3, 157
Canadian nationality, 126, 128, 174 n. 21
Canadian point of view, 4–6 (defined), 26–7

Carlyle, Thomas, 4, 11, 15, 17, 79, 84, 86, 106, 154, 156, 165 n. 13; Carlylean hero, 47, 79, 155; *Sartor Resartus*, 22, 46
Chamberlain, Joseph, 15, 112, 129, 172 n. 14
Character types, 151
Coleman, Kit, 60
Colonial point of view, 4 (defined), 6, 18, 22, 154, 158; in *Cousin Cinderella*, 26–7; of women, 37
Commercial union (with US), 15
Confederation, 13, 44
Confederation poets, 81
Connor, Ralph, 126
Conrad, Joseph, 9
Conservative Party (Canada), 113
Cultural stereotypes, 158
Curzon, George Nathaniel (Viceroy), 81, 95–6

Darwin, Charles, 123, 140, 141, 167 n. 19
Democracy, 11, 79–100; in Canada, 79–80, 82–3; critique of, 82, 156; effect on Indian government, 90–1, 92, 94; and empire, 83; in India, 146; in the US, 83